GARDEN SECRETS

Debby Peck

Nimbus
PUBLISHING

Copyright © Debby Peck, 2000

All rights reserved. No part of this book may be reproduced, stored in a retrieval system or transmitted in any form or by any means without the prior written permission from the publisher, or, in the case of photocopying or other reprographic copying, permission from CANCOPY (Canadian Copyright Licensing Agency), 1 Yonge Street, Suite 1900, Toronto, Ontario M5E 1E5.

Nimbus Publishing Limited
PO Box 9301, Station A
Halifax, NS   B3K 5N5
(902) 455-4286

Design: Graphic Detail Inc.
Printed and bound in Canada

Canadian Cataloguing in Publication Data

Peck, Debby.

    Garden Secrets
    ISBN 1-55109-348-0

1. Gardening — New Brunswick — Handbook, manuals, etc.   2. Gardening — New Brunswick — Miscellanea.   I. Title.

SB451.36.C3P42 2000   635'.09715'1   C00-950196-7

Canadä

Nimbus Publishing acknowledges financial support for our publishing activities from the Government of Canada through the Book Publishing Industry Development Program (BPIDP), and the Canada Council.

CONTENTS

Introduction VI

Garden Landscapes 1
- Elizabeth MacFarlane and Larry Wisniewski, New Maryland
- Annette and Byron McCoy, Lower St. Marys
- The secrets of a garden landscape
- Order of bloom for popular perennials
- Hardy perennial groundcover for lawn substitutes

Trees & Shrubs 7
- Jake and Betty Ann McMackin, Island View
- Phyllis Willet, Rothesay
- Kit and Fred Everett, Island View
- Dale Calder, Campobello
- A trio of flowering shrubs: February daphne, forsythia, lilac
- Roses: queen of flowers
- The secrets of gardening with trees & shrubs

Perennials 19
- Barbara Telford, Upper Gagetown
- Madeline Gibson, St. Stephen
- Judy and Bill Whalen, Quispamsis
- Reno and Beatrice Long, Grand Falls
- Brenda and Richard Toth, Bathurst
- Kim Hovey, Carlow
- Murray Alexander, Welshpool
- Diane Richard, Grand Falls
- Deanna Baldwin, Welshpool
- The secrets of gardening with perennials
- A trio of sturdy perennials: hosta, hollyhock, loosestrife
- Creating a butterfly garden

Annuals 41
- Vivian Wilcox, Nashwaaksis
- Stephen Stephenson, Jacksonville
- Beverly Corey, Welshpool
- Mary White, Carlow
- The secrets of gardening with annuals
- Good garden flowers for drying
- Edible annuals

Fruit 51
- Margie Ann and Dalbert Boyd, Douglas
- Bob Osborne, Corn Hill
- Ken Peck, Island View
- David and Susan Walker, Fredericton
- Daryl Hunter, Keswick Ridge
- The secrets of gardening with fruit
- Favourite fruit recipes

Vegetables 63
- Ted Wiggans, Frog Lake
- Peter and Marilyn Cronk, North Head, Grand Manan
- Thea Visbach, Prince William
- The secrets of gardening with vegetables
- Companion planting
- Favourite vegetable recipes

Garden Secrets

Herbs 73
- Howard Erb and Marilyn LaFrance, Cambridge
- Aaron and Anna Randall, Mouth of Keswick
- Valerie Marr, King's Landing, Prince William
- Darlene Love, Kingston
- The secrets of gardening with herbs
- A selection of herbs

How to Keep Deer out of the Garden 82
- Deer-resistant plants

Rock Gardens 85
- Erwin Landauer, Sisson Ridge
- Wilma Allair, North Road, Campobello
- Hal Hinds, Fredericton
- The secrets of rock gardens
- Suitable plants for rock gardens

Water Gardens 93
- Gail Taylor, St. George
- Rod Lutes, Alma
- John and Lola Miller, Bathurst
- The secrets of water gardens

Public Gardens 101
- Kingsbrae Horticultural Garden, St. Andrews
- Suggestions for "white garden" plants from Kingsbrae Garden: perennials, annuals, trees and shrubs.
- The New Brunswick Botanical Garden, St. Jacques
- Harbour Park, St. Martins
- Fundy Park, Alma
- Roosevelt International Park, Campobello
- The secrets of public gardens

Heritage Gardens 113
- Village Historique Acadien, Caraquet
- King's Landing Historical Settlement, Prince William
- The secrets of heritage gardens

Seed Savers 119
- Steve Stehouwer, McLeod Hill
- Kim Edmondson, Keswick Ridge
- The secrets of saving seeds
- The fermentation process

Compost—A Gardener's Best Friend 123

This book is for my favorite aunt, Barbara Reader. She always loved the outdoors and should have been able to plant many more gardens before we lost her.

INTRODUCTION

"The story of mankind began in a garden and ended in revelations."
Oscar Wilde

When I was a child, I spent a great deal of time on my grandparents' farm. There was always a large vegetable garden there, as well as a commercial apple orchard, raspberries, gooseberries, and pear and cherry trees. My decision to pursue a career as a biologist and horticulturist must have been influenced by this regular exposure to the world of plants because I can remember knowing at a very early age that I enjoyed growing things.

For the last twenty years, I have been employed at the University of New Brunswick in its Biology Department greenhouses. My workdays have been filled with planting and teaching, two of my favorite activities. I've also been a regular host of a gardening call-in program for Fredericton's CBC *Information Morning* radio broadcast, and have a seasonal gardening column in the city's newspaper, *The Daily Gleaner*. My own garden takes up more than a third of my family's six-acre property, making room for fruit trees, vegetables, herbs, perennials, and shrubs—including many of the varieties found in *Garden Secrets*.

Throughout my years as a gardener and a garden writer, I've known the great privilege of meeting delightful people who share my love of growing plants. Jovial discussions, pleasant tours through lovingly tended properties, and confessions of remarkable successes or memorable failures have always been part of this sharing of experiences. And now, just as so many gardeners have shared their gardening secrets with me, I'll share them with you. I'm convinced that gardening stories are meant to be told again and again.

Looking back over the process of collecting stories for this book, I continue to marvel at the warm generosity of New Brunswick gardeners. I began my research with just a few names of garden club presidents or nursery owners in various regions of the province, but I was soon given a long list of other people to contact. Gardeners everywhere have a network, it seems, and I quickly became a part of New Brunswick's gardening community. A visit to one garden led to visits to several others, and a tour of a garden was usually accompanied by gifts of seeds, plants, books, recipes, and other garden memorabilia.

This book is about New Brunswickers sharing stories of gardening and harvesting. Writing it has been a rewarding experience, and I hope you'll enjoy the result.

KNOW YOUR "HARDINESS ZONE"

Every plant has its limits. If it can thrive through repeated exposure to wind and sun, poor soil conditions, short growing seasons, lack of water, or poor snow cover in the winter, a plant is definitely rugged—but it isn't necessarily "hardy" in all regions of the country. A plant's hardiness, by definition, refers to its ability to survive through the coldest winter conditions in its growing location. Since the 1940s, every horticultural plant in North America has been calibrated to correspond with a "hardiness zone" based on average, annual minimum temperatures. There are nine hardiness zones in Canada, each of which has been assigned a number. In the north, the hardiness

As a gardener and garden writer, author Debby Peck visits many New Brunswick gardens, like that of Barbara Telford in Upper Gagetown.

zone may be 1 or 2 because of extremely harsh winter conditions; however, on the south shore of Nova Scotia, the hardiness zone could be 6 or 7 due to the warming influence of the ocean. In New Brunswick, hardiness zones range from 3 in Dalhousie or Edmunston to 5 in some areas along the shores of the Bay of Fundy.

Although many local variations in weather conditions can't be easily reflected on a hardiness-zone map, a plant is usually listed in the coldest zone where it will grow well. Gardeners should know the number if their own hardiness zone, and should make a habit of checking plant labels before making a purchase, to be sure they're choosing a plant that's appropriate for their zone.

Annette and Byron McCoy, Lower St. Marys

GARDEN LANDSCAPES

"She was standing inside the secret garden. It was the sweetest, most mysterious-looking place anyone could imagine…and she felt she had found a world all her own."

Frances Hodgson Burnett, *The Secret Garden*

A home landscape can be as varied as the dreams, imagination, and lifestyle of its creator. Typically, there are a number of shrubs and trees planted around the foundation of the house, either to hide the ugliness of concrete walls or to act as a privacy screen. Then there could be hedges to delineate property lines, climbing vines to cover the side of a garage or utility shed, shade trees, perennial borders, vegetable plots, rock gardens, or annual beds for summer colour. Adventurous gardeners might include a rose garden and a pond in their landscape plan, or try their hand at growing fruit trees, strawberries, or hardy grapes. And most of these garden features would be surrounded by grass. For centuries, home landscapes have focused on an outdoor carpet of green to provide that manicured look of the civilized dwelling place. Throughout history, more time, effort, and cash has been spent on the creation and upkeep of a lawn than on any other component of a landscape. When people think about doing their landscaping, they usually think about getting grass to grow. Only after the lawn is ready do they think about other plants or landscape structures.

There *is* something quite appealing about a lush green lawn, especially if it's free of weeds and doesn't have the brown patches that are evidence of an infestation of chinch bugs or other pests. But for many an avid gardener, the effort required to keep a lawn in immaculate shape means time away from the perennials or the roses or the vegetable plot. A lawn is a monoculture, after all, and nature abhors a monoculture, always trying to blow in some dandelion, chickweed, or plantain seeds. To maintain a lawn, these "weeds" have to be kept in check with a regular application of herbicide or by constant hand weeding.

In addition, a lawn needs to be constantly cut (with a noisy mower), nourished regularly, and watered frequently. And a lawn is the first thing in landscape to show signs of neglect when the homeowner goes on vacation.

More and more often, a limited lawn landscape is being considered by modern homeowners. When there is little lawn to mow, a gardener can devote more time to the rest of their landscape. There is room for inspired design. There is room for mixing and matching and personal expression. For the following gardeners, lawns were not the only option. They wanted to try something different.

ELIZABETH MACFARLANE AND LARRY WISNIEWSKI
NEW MARYLAND

When Larry Wisniewski and Elizabeth MacFarlane bought their home in New Maryland in the snowy winter of 1991, they were assured that the backyard was fully landscaped. So you can imagine their distress when the snow melted to reveal a horrible mess of fallen limbs, dead branches, and tree stumps—lots of tree stumps. It was a jungle of woody debris. Rather than digging new planting beds for perennials, rather than working at the pond they'd planned to put in along one edge of the property, they were now faced with a gardener's nightmare. There

Larry Wisniewski and Elizabeth MacFarlane transformed a mess of dead branches and tree stumps into this New Maryland garden.

wasn't a blade of grass to be seen, a speck of workable soil, or even a level piece of ground in the entire backyard. It was obvious that planting would have to wait, and that some major grubbing work would have to begin.

Elizabeth and Larry started with the stumps...all fifty of them. Larry considered the removal task to be a personal challenge that meant hacking and prying with pick-axe and crow bar. It just didn't seem right to him to consider bringing in a bulldozer to do the job, because he and Elizabeth knew that the delicate ferns and native wildflowers poking their way up through the jumble of brush would be completely eliminated if such a large piece of machinery was let loose in their garden-to-be.

As each stump was removed, Larry amended the resulting hole's soil with imported black earth and composted chicken manure. Slowly but surely the ground was levelled, gravel-covered paths were created, and rock-rimmed beds were readied for planting. The pond was finally dug and surrounded with flagstone. Bird and butterfly feeders were put in place and a gargoyle or two were invited to sit among the plants, just to keep an eye on things.

During this industrious activity, a magnificent stone wall was built to enclose the entire garden. On trips to walk their dogs along back country roads, Elizabeth and Larry filled the trunk of their car with stones of interesting sizes and shapes, each of which was destined to be added to their garden wall. It took several years to complete, but the final product is a fence around the whole backyard, and a structure that not only provides a perfect frame for their tranquil planting scheme, but a rugged enclosure that reminds visitors of the functional stone walls used to rim Maritime farmlands in years gone by.

When asked about favourites in their plant collection, Larry and Elizabeth both admit to being particularly partial to lilies. An entire bed at the back of the garden has been devoted to a collection of Asiatic lilies that bloom orange, yellow, red, pink, and white. Lilies are also tucked into dozens of other pockets throughout the garden; these include the cultivars Star Gazer, Casablanca, and a couple of spectacular, white-flowered Madonna. Several Canada lilies rescued from a road construction site near the Saint John River now grow to heights of five or six feet, each one producing dozens of bell-shaped orange blossoms in early summer.

Elsewhere in this wonderful backyard, a herb bed contains woolly and variegated thyme, mint, lavender, feverfew, St. John's wort, beebalm, and wormwood. A monochromatic garden is planted with white-blooming varieties of liatris, shasta daisy, violets, spiderwort, and astilbe, amid a contrasting foliage of silver mound artemisia and a Gentle Shepherd daylily that has delicate, white blossoms in mid-June. A large and showy collection of the old-fashioned, low-maintenance, orange-flowered daylilies has been planted near the pond. These are flanked by moisture-loving Siberian and Japanese iris, and the native "blue-flag" iris. The beauty of daylilies and iris is that even after plants have finished blooming, their attractive, sword-like foliage remains lush and appealing.

Larry and Elizabeth have planted hardy roses from the Explorer series in beds of various shapes and sizes through the central part of the backyard. These are combined with sun-loving perennials such as purple coneflower, lysimachia, ajuga, leopard's bane, hollyhocks, peonies, foxglove, delphiniums, and evening primroses. At the back corner of the property, under a light-filtering canopy of birch and pine, a shade garden is home to ligularia, astilbe, hosta, and ferns, which mingle with wildflowers like bluebeard lily and solomon's seal. Many of these beds are outlined with stones, and all are mulched with shredded bark and connected by paths of crushed gravel.

Grassy patches surround the base of large trees, or form the path between beds. "But they're just a garden waiting to happen," says Elizabeth. And some lawn does remain at the front of the house, between a herbaceous perennial border that runs along the walkway to the front door and another collection of perennials planted in a bed that stretches the width of the property, parallel to the street. This small section of lawn takes very little time to mow and gives the couple's Labrador retrievers a free space to stretch out in the sun. But who knows how long it will be there? Grass has never lasted long in this landscape!

Annette and Byron McCoy
Lower St. Marys

Even though traffic usually travels at a good clip along the Trans-Canada Highway through New Brunswick's Lower St. Marys, a quick glance is all that's needed for a passerby to realize that there's something unique about the property belonging to Annette and Byron McCoy. But such a glimpse is certainly not enough to take everything in, and that's the reason for this story. The McCoy's landscape plan began to take shape in 1995, when Annette decided that she was awfully tired of looking at the expanse of weedy grass that had always stretched between the front of her house and the road. So, with Byron's help, she made a garden out of the whole area, complete with perennials bordering meandering walkways, a collection of flowering shrubs and evergreen trees, a water garden, and a quiet seating circle to relax in at the end of the gardening day. It was a long process. The first year, the couple took out the existing lawn and worked twenty bales of old hay into the soil to improve its organic matter content. The second year, after deciding where planting beds would be placed and where walking paths would be created, they put in shrubs and trees as accent plants, many of which Annette had started from seed. She wanted evergreens to add winter

Annette McCoy interspersed whimsical relics all through her garden in Lower St. Marys.

colour, form, and foliage texture; a bird's nest spruce and several pyramidal cedars filled the bill. She also wanted shrubs with colourful leaves, and picked golden elderberry. For woody plants with interesting stem shades, she picked variegated dogwood. And for shrubs with intensely-fragrant flowers, she planted a mock orange and lots of roses.

It wasn't until the third summer that Annette finally put a spade into the soil to begin planting annuals and perennials. These were meticulously placed for a combination that would be a treat to the eye. Annette didn't stick to any one theme, but kept colour schemes consistent, and placed plants in such a way that she'd have a great view from the front windows of her home. She also tried hard to group varieties of perennials so that something would always be in bloom around the yard. Plants with grey and silver foliage—like dianthus and veronica—added accent and contrast to various shades of green. Favourite herbs like apple mint and wormwood were planted throughout the garden for visual appeal as well as for culinary and medicinal uses. She planted vines and climbers (like morning glories, clematis, and hops), supporting their growth on cylinders of chicken wire or on tripods made from dead birch and poplar branches. In her perennial bed, she seeded a few corn plants, just because she likes the look of the plants' upright stalk and broad, drooping leaves. One of her hobbies is creating everlasting arrangements, so she made sure to have flowers that dry well, like lady's mantle and bleeding heart. The garden teems with heirloom plants like peonies, lungwort, and delphiniums, as well as brightly-coloured annuals like ornamental cabbage, impatiens, and self-sowing poppies.

Finally, Annette interspersed whimsical relics all through the garden. There are two four-legged bathtubs, for example. One sits directly under an old-fashioned hand pump that actually produces water when properly primed. The other tub sits in a depression of perfectly-placed stones, which form the bottom of Annette's water garden. A recirculating pump keeps water supplied to the basin of the tub and allows it to trickle over the edge into the rock-lined pool.

To make her routine garden maintenance a bit easier, Annette keeps water-filled buckets throughout the landscape so she can quickly refresh a drooping peony or a wilted delphinium. Apple baskets, to hold weeds and other garden debris, are also scattered around the garden; Byron fills the water buckets and empties the apple baskets every evening.

Together, they put up a greenhouse in 1994, heating it with a wood stove and using it each spring to get a head start on plants for their garden. When Annette first moves her greenhouse seedlings into the garden, she sets them under inverted strawberry boxes to provide a bit of shade and wind protection until they acclimatize to their garden home.

Annette gets her love of gardening from her mother, who was a graduate of the Ontario Agricultural College in Guelph. In fact, the McCoy's garden has some "keepsake plants"—a special lilac bush, for example—that are descendants of specimens from her mother's Shetland, Ontario home. She also has plants from friends and neighbours; these have a special place in her collection and are just part of what Annette thinks is one of the nicest parts of gardening: sharing plants with others.

The Secrets of a Garden Landscape

- Choose shrubs and trees to form the framework of your garden landscape.
- Pick shrubs and trees with interesting stem and leaf colours or with fragrant blossoms.
- Consider shrubs and perennials that flower at different times in the season so that there is always something in bloom.
- Make mass plantings of daylilies and iris, which have lovely foliage after they finish blooming.
- Intersperse plants with meandering stone walkways, collections of boulders, or gravel paths.
- Make room for sculptures and whimsical garden artifacts.
- Keep tools handy by placing storage bins directly in the garden.
- Place large, water-filled buckets at convenient places around the garden to make it easy to revive a thirsty plant.

Order of Bloom for Popular Perennials

Month of Bloom	Botanical Name	Common Name
Late April	Arabis caucasica	rock cress
Early to mid-May	Bergenia cardifolia	turtle leaf
	Doronicum cordatus	leopard's bane
	Primula polyantha	polyantha primrose
	Viola (various species)	blue or white violets
	Pulmonaria officinalis	lungwort
	Iberis saxatilis	rock candytuft
Late May to early June	Dicentra spectabilis	bleeding heart
	Dianthus plumarius	cottage pink
	Aquilegia hybrida	columbine
	Heuchera sanguinea	coral bells
	Primula japonica	Japanese primrose
	Lupinus officinalis	lupine
	Hemerocallis fulva	tawny daylily
	Polemonium caeruleum	Jacob's ladder
Late June	Papaver orientale	oriental poppy
	Trollius (various species)	buttercup or globe flower
	Leucanthemum superbum	shasta daisy
	Iris sp.	bearded iris
	Lavendula officinalis	lavender
	Clematis sp.	clematis
	Lilium sp.	lily
	Achillea millefolium	yarrow
	Alchemilla mollis	lady's mantle
	Thymus serphyllum	creeping/mother of thyme
	Thymus pseudolanuginosus	woolly thyme
	Lysimachia punctata	yellow loosestrife
	Paeonia officinalis	peony
	Penstemon digitalis	penstemon
July	Hosta sp.	plantain lily
	Aconitum napellus	monkshood
	Tradescantia virginiana	spiderwort
	Echinacea purpurea	purple coneflower
	Hypericum perforatum	St. John's wort
	Echinops ritro	globe thistle
	Lychnis chalcedonica	Maltese Cross
	Veronica spicata	veronica
	Filapendula ulmaria	Queen of the meadow
	Lilium canadense	Canada lily
	Monarda didyma	beebalm
	Gypsophila paniculata	baby's breath
	Valeriana officinalis	valerian
	Althaea rosea	hollyhock
	Astilbe arendsii	astilbe
	Ligularia dentata	Othello rayflower
	Ligularia stenocephala	rocket rayflower
	Platycodon grandiflorum	balloon flower
	Liatris scariosa	gayfeather
	Physostegia virginiana	obedient plant
August	Asclepias tuberosa	butterfly weed
	Rudbeckia sullivantii	black-eyed Susan
	Helenium autumnale	sneezeweed
	Aster nolvi-belgii	Michaelmas daisy
	Sedum spectabile	autumn joy sedum

Hardy Perennial Groundcover for Lawn Substitutes

Note: a "groundcover" is a mass planting of a single type of plant that spreads quickly to cover the ground with thick foliage.

Botanical Name	Common Name
Geranium sp.	cranesbill
Lysimachia nummularia	creeping Jenny
Vinca minor	periwinkle vine
Thymus serpyllum	thyme
Lamium maculatum	lamium
Ajuga reptans	bugle weed
Atennaria sp.	pussytoes
Cotoneaster adpressa	creeping cotoneaster
Pachysandra procumbens	Japanese spurge
Juniperus horizontalis	creeping juniper
Convallaria majalis	lily-of-the-valley

Phyllis Willet, Rothesay

Trees & Shrubs

"If a tree dies, plant another in its place."

Linnaeus, 1707-1778

othing gives a garden a sense of permanence and completeness more than trees. The placing of trees in a landscape lends the impression of foresight and commitment and a promise for years to come. This may sound a bit eccentric, but when you plant a tree, you do so with the understanding that it will take quite some time before it reaches its full potential—you're planning for the future.

Because trees and shrubs are perennial plants, they should be chosen carefully and placed appropriately. I'm often asked how to prune a tree that's "getting too big for where it's planted." It's usually not the tree's fault; it may be a specimen known to have a mature height that is now much too tall for its chosen location. But when the gardener first purchased these specimens, they were just small things that looked perfect in those particular sites.

Pruning an ornamental conifer like Colorado Blue Spruce, just because it's too close to the front step, always ruins its wonderful natural shape. And cutting back a Crimson King maple just because its canopy has reached the eaves of the house is a good way to ruin the growth of an attractive tree.

The same is true for shrubs and pruning. Although some shrubs (like roses and hydrangea) respond well to a regular haircut, others (like rhododendrons and azaleas) do poorly when they have their growth checked on an annual basis. And many shrubs produce wonderful flowers that will be completely eliminated if plants are pruned at the wrong time of the year.

However, when trees and shrubs are planted and pruned correctly, they can become focal points on the lawn—or incorporated into a collection of herbaceous perennials, adding an element of height and breadth to a flower border. Or they can be hedges and screens. They can also provide privacy and shade. In other words, they have a place in just about any garden setting.

My own garden is surrounded by dozens of varieties of trees. Mature specimens of spruce, fir, hemlock, poplar, and birch grow in the wooded areas behind the house, along with a dozen butternut trees that we share with squirrels (although these four-legged nut hounds usually beat us to the mark when the butternuts start falling to the ground each autumn). A line of nine mature rock maples along the driveway turns a fabulous shade of orange-red at the end of the growing season, and there are lots of eastern white cedar growing around natural springs that dot the property.

To accompany these trees, I planted a wide variety of shrubs, chosen for their bloom times, their leaf and stem colours, their flower types, and their forms. Old-fashioned mauve lilacs are transplants from my mother's garden, and a dwarf Korean lilac has intensely purple blossoms. There is a burning bush, a variegated leafed dogwood, a bridal wreath spirea, a bittersweet vine, and a ninebark, along with rhododendrons, honeysuckle, and weeping caragana. Shrubs like high-bush cranberries, elderberries, and wild raisin attract birds, and there are lots of hardy roses—both climbers like New Dawn and Henry Kelsey, and tough, shrubbier types like Jens Munk, Blanc Double de Coubert, and Therese Bugnet. I love roses and try to add to my collection each year. With a little knowledge—like that of the following gardeners—you'll find that trees and shrubs have much to offer.

Jake and Betty Ann McMackin
Island View

Jake and Betty Ann McMackin have been growing roses for a long time. Some of the varieties in the collection at their Island View home are more than twenty years old—and not because these plants are hardy and need little attention. Quite the contrary: the McMackin rose garden is an exhibit of hybrid tea roses that needs regular care to not only ensure production of this "queen of flowers," but also to guarantee each plant's survival through a cold Canadian winter. To some, rose gardening can seem frustrating and time consuming, but for avid rose lovers like the McMackins, growing hybrid teas is a labour of love. They know their efforts will be returned many times in exquisite blossoms and delectable fragrances, and one glimpse of their garden provides the proof!

Hybrid tea roses are probably the most popular group of roses grown in modern times because they generally bloom all summer long. Low and bushy, their large, long-stemmed flowers make wonderful bouquets. Available through mail order and at garden centres or nurseries, hybrid tea roses are usually sold in colourful cardboard boxes, with their roots wrapped in a bag of moist peat moss or wood shavings, and their leafless, thorny branches coated with wax to prevent desiccation. In the last half century, rose breeders have produced thousands of new hybrid tea varieties from which to choose, all with exquisite flowers. However, because of their tender nature, gardeners often treat them as annual bedding plants. But hybrid tea roses can survive from year to year in the colder parts of North America, if some special techniques for winter protection are understood.

Putting their roses to bed for the winter is something that Jake and Betty Ann McMackin are experts at. They usually begin the project just after Remembrance Day, when their rose

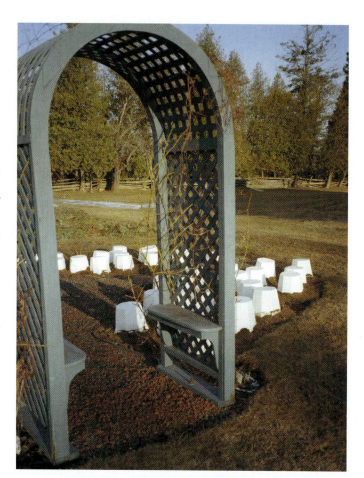

The McMackins use "rose caps" to protect their rose bushes from the wind and cold of a New Brunswick winter.

plants are dormant and have been the subject of several weeks of heavy frost. First comes pruning. This involves removing any dead wood from each plant and cutting back its branches to about eight inches from the ground. A styrofoam "rose cap" is then placed over the plant and anchored in place with a bit of soil piled around its base. Rose caps look like an octagonal planter, but they're meant to be inverted over a rose bush to provide protection from cold and wind throughout the winter. Durable and storable from one season to the next, you'll find them at hardware stores and garden centres. According to the McMackins, rose caps have made end-of-season chores for hybrid tea rose growers a bit less intensive. However, even though the caps provide quick-to-install insulation, they work best with an accompanying snow cover; some years, the McMackins lose a few of their rose cap-covered plants, blaming it on the fact that New Brunswick sometimes has little snow on the ground.

Rose caps can be a bit of an investment for anyone who has a large collection of plants. Because they grow more than 50 hybrid teas, the McMackins have decided to purchase just a few new caps each year. That means that they continue to use the old-fashioned way of overwintering some of their roses. After they finish their capping work, they start to dig up the rest of their collection, transferring it from the garden to a special storage box that Jake constructed. The box's bottom is simply a rectangular wooden frame that's partially buried in a sheltered spot at the back of the McMackin property. The box's sides are made of styrofoam-lined pieces of plywood that hook together to form an enclosure approximately five feet long, three feet wide, and three feet high.

After the roses are dug from the garden and wrapped in sheets of burlap, Betty Ann places them in the storage box and covers them with a deep layer of loose, free-draining soil and a bit of fungicide. Then the insulated lid is placed on the box, making it ready to protect the McMackins' roses all winter.

In the spring, after all danger of frost is past, Jake and Betty Ann remove their rose caps and retrieve the plants that have overwintered in the storage box. When everything is replanted in their rose garden for another season, they soon enjoy the sight of fresh new shoots bursting forth from healthy plants. It's a joy to behold each time and makes the fall work worth it.

Phyllis Willet
Rothesay

When the owner of a newly-built home begins the task of landscaping the property, decisions have to be made about what types of plants will be used and where they should be placed. To accompany the installation of lawn and flower beds, trees and shrubs have to be selected, and thought given to where they will best provide privacy, wind break, colour, and visual appeal from the house or street.

This type of landscape planning was on the mind of Phyllis Willet and her family when they first moved into their new home, high on a bluff overlooking the beautiful Kennebecasis River on the fringes of the city of Saint John. The property sloped gently away from the street, and the house was situated to take advantage of the impressive view of the water below.

The park-like setting was a perfect place for a showcase of shrubbery. With the help of Don Miller, a landscaper from nearby St. Martins who had studied at the school of horticulture at Guelph University in Ontario, Phyllis began collecting and planting a variety of evergreens—including some rare and unusual imported pines, spruces, cotoneasters, heathers, and ornamental maples. She clustered them together in what she refers to as her "conifer garden," which sits atop a knoll in the lawn, with an inviting set of flagstone steps and benches. The species in this remarkable grouping have many different needle and leaf colours, and a variety of shapes and forms. As they matured over the years, they filled in the spaces originally left between them, making a year-round screen from the street, and a focal point on the property.

In 1980, Phyllis decided she'd like a rhododendron garden, because she was intrigued by their gorgeous flowers and interesting foliage. Rhododendrons and their sister plants, the azaleas, are members of the *Ericaceae* family of plants; they prefer to grow in acid soils and in partial shade. Phyllis's planting location of choice was on the river side of the house, where she felt the rhododendrons could be best admired from large picture windows and a deck. However, the soil in that spot was poor and full of huge rocks and boulders. To create a suitable planting area, she and a landscaper had to clear away stones and then bring in what seemed like vast quantities of peat moss.

The first rhododendron specimens came from a nursery in Nova Scotia: Nova Zembla, which has red flowers and is known to tolerate the cold winters and hot summers typical in New Brunswick; Francesca, which have dramatic, wine-red blossoms; Boule de Neige, an early, white-blooming variety; and a number of Yakusimanum, fondly referred to by Phyllis as the "Yaks." The latter are super hardy with pale, white-coloured blossoms, a dwarf growth habit, and great insect and disease resistance. With the rhododendrons came several types of azaleas, including Tuscan with its pale, orange, fragrant blossoms; and the winter-hardy Klondike, which has strikingly bright yellow-orange flowers.

Over time, the rhododendrons became too crowded. They grew less vigorously and started to flower less frequently. Branches became tangled and leaves got smaller. That's when Phyllis's daughter Sharan undertook the task of a complete makeover for the rhododendron beds. She moved duplicate plants and the sickest to another site on the property, then spread out the existing plants, grouping together varieties with similar flower colour and growth form. New varieties were added, like the low-growing Purple Jem and the popular P.J.M. hybrid, and a grass path was made through the middle of the bed for easier access to plants at the bottom of the garden. Since the bed renovation, Sharan has made sure that the rhododendrons are properly fertilized in the spring with a slow-release fertilizer, that flower clusters are removed just as they start to fade each year, and that plants are well watered during the hottest part of the summer, when their hillside location becomes exceedingly dry. Sharan also makes sure that the entire bed is properly protected for the winter by placing a huge burlap fence around its perimeter each fall. The result of this care and attention is apparent, especially in late May and early June, when the rhododendrons are in full bloom.

The trees and shrubs gracing the Willet landscape are a fine example of an appropriate planting design. They enhance the property and bring much joy to their owners—just what plants, with a little planning, will always do.

KIT AND FRED EVERETT
ISLAND VIEW

For almost two centuries, there have been Everetts farming high on a hilltop in Island View, New Brunswick. In fact, the property is part of a land grant to the current owner's great-great-great grandfather. Over the years, there have been changes to the crops planted and to the livestock tended, but the essential setting has always remained the same: fertile ground and a magnificent view of the islands and thoroughfares of the Saint John River Valley, just west of Fredericton. From the front door of the farmhouse, you can gaze north over the river to a panorama of hills and forest. From the back of the barnyard stretch acres of pasture and woodland. It's truly a beautiful spot—one that was a welcome sight for Kit Everett when she and her husband Fred moved back in 1963 to manage the farm.

For the first years of their marriage, Kit and Fred had lived in a number of different places while he served in the air force, completed his studies, and took a research scientist position at the Agriculture Station in Fredericton. Kit had very little opportunity to garden in all of those places, for one reason or another, but she knew things were about to change. "It was the unlimited land that appealed to me" she remembers, when she first decided to start a garden at the farm. But with so much space, it was hard to know where to begin.

It was obvious that the first requirement would be some sort of boundary to delineate her own cultivation from the vast expanse of farm fields, pasture, and orchards that surrounded the house and barns. She admits that Fred, "who has always had a great eye for design," suggested she should use shrubbery instead of fences to form the backbone of the garden. "He could look ahead to see what the garden would become," Kit acknowledges, "and he knew that shrubs would have a role to play."

"It was the unlimited land that appealed to me," recalls Kit Everett, when she and husband Fred first decided to start a garden.

They looked for a source of planting material to fit their needs, and decided their best bet was to order from a catalogue. "These trees were offered in one of those mail-order nursery catalogues from Ontario that sold twenty-five of this and twenty-five of that," says Fred, when recalling how they went about the process. "They were so small and so pretty when they first arrived!" He put them all in a temporary bed until they were needed in the landscape. Some weren't transplanted to their final growing place for at least five years—the time it took for house renovations and landscape sculpturing—but eventually all the plants were put in place around what was to become the garden. Now that almost forty years has passed, and those shrubs and trees have matured, it's obvious that the Everetts made the right choices all those years ago.

Kit and Fred's garden wraps itself nicely all around their house but is most intensely planted in areas that are easily visible from the living room and sunroom windows. Directly against the foundation are several spreading junipers, some columnar and globe cedar, and two varieties of japanese yew. These trees are magnificently pruned, nestling up against the house without blocking the view from windows and doors. None have been fertilized with much more than a bit of compost over the years, because Fred has been trying to keep them from getting too big. In fact, one huge juniper adjacent to the front step has actually outgrown its usefulness and is going to be taken out—it's so big that Fred is sure he'll need a tractor to do the job!

Two pyramidal cedar near the edge of the vegetable garden have lately been left to themselves. Fred used to be able to prune their tops to keep their growth in check, but in the last few years they've become too tall for his ladder, so he lets them grow without restriction. "I've wrapped some coated wire around some of the branches that tend to fall outwards from the main trunk," he says, "and then I anchor them back in towards the center, so they don't get broken off by wind or snow." He admits "that's something to consider when planting a shrub—it can get too big for the location, at some point." Fred suggests that growing dwarf types is always a good idea, particularly in small spaces.

Kit's perennial beds are woven between patches of lawn between the house and the apple orchard. A stately blue spruce and several cedars stand out as backdrops, along with a weeping crab that Fred grafted over twenty years ago. The crab tree is stunning in early spring, when it's in full bloom, and, in late fall and through the winter, its fruit draw cedar waxwings. "They stay around until they eat every last crab apple on the tree" says Fred, who enjoys bird-watching from a comfortable chair in the living room, after the gardening season is over.

And then there is the "Transcendent" crab tree which became incorporated into the garden design at the very beginning. It was hard to do anything else, really, because the tree is over a century old and was on the property when Fred was a boy. The tree's trunk is gnarled with age, and its branches cascade down to the lawn. "We still harvest the fruit," he says, although the tree seems to produce in cycles, bearing a better harvest in some years than in others.

Along with the evergreens, Kit and Fred planted many varieties of flowering shrubs and woody vines as accent plants. Some are on a lovely arbour, built for a garden party celebration on Canada's 125th birthday. "Kit has planted more things at the base of that arbour," grins Fred. "But I think the grapes might be losing out to other things." He's referring to the honeysuckle and clematis that Kit expected to share this garden spot with a grape of an unknown heritage. "It's a small fruited variety that dies back to the ground each winter and looks like a dead duck each spring," she explains. But the grape has looked this way at the start of every garden season since it was planted almost ten years ago. It always puts on such growth that it completely covers its side of the arbour, holding its own against neighbouring plants and always producing a harvest. Another grape, growing by itself on a sturdy trellis at the back of the garage, is much older with a trunk that's many centimetres in diameter. "It's been here for over a century," says Kit, "and it makes the very best jelly!"

Along a back edge of the perennial border is an American larch, pruned into a mounded shape. Its needles turn yellow in the fall, making it a prize specimen, and even after they drop off it's a lovely sight with its knobbed branches and tiny cones. Then there are the roses, placed to add fragrance and foliage contrast to the rest of the garden. Some are unnamed, like one with small pink-flowers, growing in a large clump on the lawn adjacent to the sunroom door. With thornless stems and small leaves, it's one of Fred's favourites, and he has christened it "the Graduation Rose" because it always blooms just in time for high school graduation each spring.

Another rose in the Everett garden is an Adelaide Hoodless, a hardy, disease-resistant, repeat bloomer with a beautiful red blossom. It's a special favourite of Kit's because it's named after the founder of the Women's Institute in Canada, where she has been a member for many years.

The trees and shrubs around the Everett's garden have reached a maturity that suits the heritage of the farmscape that surrounds them, and have served their purpose well as a significant feature in this garden. "In the spring, when there is so little growth from anything else in the garden, I look out and am especially pleased with their presence," says Kit. "They look strong and vigorous in the stillness of the season."

Dale Calder
Campobello

Dale Calder has spent the past twenty years creating an ornamental forest in his garden on Campobello Island. His nine-acre property is sheltered on all sides by common tree species native to New Brunswick (it falls into a hardiness zone 5); here, Dale has been planting exotic species not often seen in the rest of the province. "I love to experiment with material that's barely hardy here," he admits, "just for the challenge of pushing the limits." "Gardening to the extreme" might be one way of describing his planting philosophy, and when there is success it's that much sweeter. "If I kept a list of what I've lost over the years because it didn't survive our winters, it would be very long," he confesses. But what he has been able to grow is astonishing, and is an education for New Brunswick gardeners who've always restricted themselves to planting trees and shrubs that will survive in hardiness Zones 2 to 4.

Dale has planted some of the most interesting woody plants right around the foundation of his house. At the front, a Jackman's clematis climbs up a latticed arbour that surrounds the door frame; it's one of ten different clematis species in Dale's garden. Known botanically as *Clematis* x *jackmanii*, this rewarding vine has large, purple blossoms that appear, in eastern Canada,

Dale Calder planted trees and shrubs around the foundation of his home on Campobello Island.

in mid-July. The species was selected by English plant breeder George Jackman in 1858, and it remains one of the most popular of all clematis. "I never do a thing to it," says Dale. Nor does he need to give much attention to another species, which climbs up the house near the back door. It's a *Clematis tangutica*, commonly called the "golden" clematis because of its bright yellow flowers. It's an autumn bloomer, with gorgeous, lush foliage during the summer. "I took a garden rake to it recently, to thin it out a bit," says Dale. "But that was just to check its growth a bit." Like the Jackman variety, a golden clematis blooms on the previous year's wood, and usually requires no more maintenance than annual removal of dead or broken branches. However, they do appreciate having their roots kept cool, so it's best to either plant them close to a low-growing perennial (to take advantage of the shade provided by that plant's foliage), or to mulch the base of the clematis with a thick layer of shredded bark or wood chips.

At the front of Dale's house, just adjacent to the Jackman clematis, is a weeping mulberry tree with an interesting history: mulberries were introduced to Britain from China about four hundred years ago, for the silk industry. Silk worms feed on the leaves of the white mulberry (*Morus alba*), a round-topped, dense tree that produces fruit similar in size and shape to blackberries. The plant is hardy to zone 4 (if not exposed to harsh winter winds on a regular basis) and weeping forms, like Dale's Morus alba 'Kingan' are resistant to drought and salt spray. It's a great specimen for planting in poor soils.

To balance the pendulous form of the mulberry, Dale planted a weeping caragana on the opposite side of the front door. Caragana belong to the pea family of plants, producing bright yellow flowers that mature into small pods in midsummer. They have spines of prickles at the base of the leaves, and their stiffly-drooping branches give the plant a special charm.

Near the caragana is another shrub that's uncommon in the neighbourhood: *Kerria japonica* has gracefully-arching stems of a yellowish green, which makes the plant appealing in winter months against the white of freshly-fallen snow. In summer the plant is covered with abundant tangerine-yellow blossoms that look just like little balls of fire all along the branches. Kerria is trouble free and can tolerate both sun and partial shade.

His garden is also home to a Royal Star magnolia, native to Japan, which produces fragrant, white flowers early in the growing season, each with 12 to 15 long, narrow petals. The plant only reaches heights of 1.5 metres at maturity, so it's perfect for putting in front of a border of taller shrubs and trees. It never needs pruning. "And it has successfully overwintered in my garden," says Dale, "even in years when there has been no snow cover."

But perhaps the most unusual shrub in Dale's garden is his devil's walking stick (*Aralia spinosa*). It's a tricky plant to grow because it's so hard to work around; stems are stout and grow to impressive lengths in a single season—but are covered with spines that can wound unsuspecting gardeners. There's often some die-back with the plant after the winter, though it grows again from the roots each spring.

At the base of Dale's driveway is an apple orchard with a single tree. "This is a Pumpkin Sweet type of apple," he explains, "and it's self pollinating, so I've only needed to plant one." The tree regularly produces a fine crop of large and tasty cooking apples. "They need a frost to bring out their flavour," says Dale, so he harvests them each year in mid-October.

Recent additions to Dale's ornamental forest include rhododendrons, azaleas from the Northern Lights series, a Montmorency cherry, an arctic apricot, and some interesting prostrate junipers. He has a special place for each one and enjoys the challenges of keeping them alive and healthy. But he'll always be looking for others. "I'm a bit compulsive when it comes to finding something new," he says with a glint in his eye, "And there's lots of room left in the garden."

A Trio of Flowering Shrubs that Celebrate Spring

February Daphne

A terrifically hardy shrub that's one of the earliest to bloom in a central and southern New Brunswick climate is a little bush called February daphne (*Daphne mezereum*). This short but erect shrub grows to heights of just one metre, but will spread as wide as it is tall.

The daphne is named after a lovely young nymph of Greek mythology, a spritely soul who loved to spend her days playing happily in the woods. Unfortunately, she attracted the attention of the god Apollo and became the object of his fervent pursuit. When she begged for the assistance of the other gods of the time, they responded by turning her into a shrub, which is where she continues to spend her days. Her beauty certainly shines forth, because a daphne bush is covered with tiny, rose-pink flowers even before its leaves appear each spring—blossoms so fragrant that just a single branch of blossoms will fill an entire room with its sweet smell. These flowers eventually become bright red berries that continue to decorate the plant for the rest of the growing season.

A daphne should be planted where it will receive lots of light in the early part of the day but remain out of the hot, drying rays of direct afternoon sun. And because the shrub responds badly to being moved, it's important to site it properly from the start. Just plant it, and then leave it alone. A mulch should be applied to the base of the plant to keep roots cool. Pruning is seldom necessary, but if a daphne needs a bit of shaping, it's best to do it right after the blooms fade, because the next year's flower buds are formed early in the summer, and they'll be cut off if pruning is done too late.

Forsythia

Soon after a daphne completes its delightful blooming period, Forsythia bushes take over the landscape. These stunning, spring flowering shrubs can be almost blinding in their brightness, with yellow blossoms that, like those of the daphne, appear well before the plant starts to leaf out. Forsythia was named in honour of the royal British gardener William Forsyth (1737-1804). Unfortunately, many older varieties of this long-lived and disease-free shrub are prone to winter bud damage; unless branches are well protected from extremely cold temperatures by being buried with lots of snow, the flowers will be killed during the winter months and nothing but leaves will appear in the spring. Luckily, plant breeders have recently released a new cultivar appropriately named Northern Gold. It's a dependable bloomer, even after winters with little snow cover, and it will thrive if planted in a place with lots of sunshine well-drained soil. Pruning will be necessary to keep the plant from looking gangly, but the task should be delayed until just after the shrub has flowered each year.

Lilac

The final plant in this trio of spring-blooming shrubs is the well-loved and well-known lilac (*Syringa vulgaris*). Although the most popular flower shade of this old-fashioned shrub is the traditional lilac colour, today's hybrids come in all shades of mauve, purple, and red. There are also lilacs with pure white blossoms, and with single and double flowers. Actually, the number of lilac hybrids is astounding and includes American, Chinese, French, Korean, Japanese, and Manchurian lines, all of which have different blooming times. True lilac lovers, of course, own some of each.

Lilacs grow well in full sun but will tolerate light shade. They prefer moist, well-drained soil, and will hold their blooms longer if outdoor temperatures remain cool. High nitrogen fertilizers should be avoided, because they will encourage lilacs to produce more foliage at the expense of their flowers. Pruning is best done immediately after flowering, with care to remove no more than one third of the length of the plants' branches each year. And it's important to be patient. It may take as long as six years for a lilac to reach its peak blooming age—the fragrance is worth the wait!

Roses: "Queen of Flowers"

It's difficult to say exactly when the love affair between roses and humans first began, but fossil records tell us that these gorgeous plants have been on the earth for as long as 3.5 billion years. Perhaps they were first admired in 30 B.C. when Marc Antony asked Cleopatra to strew his grave with roses. Or maybe it was in 60 A.D., when Nero ordered the equivalent of $150,000 worth of roses for a single banquet. Whatever occasion prompted our obsession with the rose, this queen of the plant world has always been associated with excitement, love, romance, and beauty. Wars have been fought in the name of roses, and family emblems have incorporated their form. The rose has travelled with colonists, been painted by famous artists, enjoyed international attention, and known the favour of many famous plant breeders and horticulturists. The national flower of England, roses are planted in private and public gardens all over the world. They are a universal symbol of nobility and grace, and there is, perhaps, no more rewarding a plant to have in your garden.

Canadians love to grow roses. Each year they plant as many as seven hundred thousand of them. And not all of these gardeners are expert rosarians—after all, roses, in one form or another, have managed to survive in a wild state in nearly every corner of the world for thousands of years. They're quite obliging when given certain growing conditions, and when the right species is chosen for a particular setting.

The proper conditions for rose growing are based first and foremost on light requirements. Most roses need at least a half day of direct sun, preferably in the morning or afternoon, rather than in the middle of the day, when bright light is accompanied with elevated temperatures. And flowers will last longer when not exposed to full sun during the hottest part of the day.

Roses require well-drained soil rich in organic matter, and their roots won't tolerate soggy, water-saturated conditions. Heavy, clay soils can grow roses if amended with compost, peat moss, well-rotted manure, and sand to improve drainage. Sandy soils are usually too low in nutrients for roses, but the addition of compost can be a big help.

Another important point to consider about rose growing is the necessity for good air circulation around the plants. Roses are prone to attack by fungal diseases, which spread quickly when bushes are planted close together. However, if fresh air can move freely around and between individual rose bushes, it's more difficult for fungal spores to spread, so adequate spacing between individual plants is a must.

Like most living things, roses do best when they receive a balanced supply of nutrients, which can be provided in either an organic or inorganic form. Gardeners who prefer to use organic fertilizers should select types high in phosphorus, and should work them into the soil several weeks in advance of planting. Roses established for a season or more will benefit from an application of organic fertilizer in both the spring and fall, when plants are dormant.

Dry chemical fertilizers can be scratched into the soil, at rates recommended on their labels, in a ring around the base of newly-planted bushes, approximately 15 cm away from the stem. Water-soluble plant foods can also be used. Both types of fertilizers should be applied after the plant has finished blooming, and then once every month until approximately six weeks before the first fall frost is anticipated. Inadequate fertilizer is usually the reason for poor blooming, and too much fertilizer can stimulate fast but weak growth, susceptible to disease and pest damage. An expert rosarian would say that "practice makes perfect" and, of course, every rose grower has his or her own secret for getting the best growth from plants.

Finally, roses grow best when properly pruned, and the best time to do that is just before leaves appear in the spring. The job should be done with sharp pruning shears and heavy gloves. Experienced rose pruners recommend making all cuts on an angle approximately 1 cm above an outward facing bud; this way, new growth will be directed to the outside of the branch rather than to the inside. Dead, damaged, or diseased tissue should be removed first, followed by shaping (if desired) so that plant growth will look symmetrical and balanced. Removing old canes (the ones with greyish thorns) will stimulate new stem growth.

Rose Petal Jelly

2 quarts rose petals, packed (from rugosa roses)
3 cups water
1 package fruit pectin crystals
2 tbsp lemon juice
4 cups sugar

Boil the water with the petals added. Stir, crushing petals against the side of the pot. Let steep for 20 to 30 minutes, stirring often, and crushing the petals each time. Strain to make three cups (add water, if necessary). Add pectin crystals and lemon juice. Boil the mixture and add the sugar. Return the mixture to a boil, while stirring, and continue boiling for one minute. Remove from heat, skim off foam, pour into sterilized jelly jars, and seal.

The Secrets of Gardening with Trees and Shrubs

- Plant rhododendrons and azaleas in areas with partial shade, mulch them with pine needles, and give them nutrients in the form of an acid fertilizer.
- Consider planting some borderline hardy trees and shrubs, especially if you have a protected garden site.
- Avoid applying excess amounts of nitrogen to lilacs, to keep them producing flowers rather than leaves.
- Remove flower clusters from rhododendrons and azaleas just after they finish blooming.
- Prune early-blooming shrubs (like forsythia, daphne, and lilac) directly after they finish flowering each year.
- Protect rhododendrons and azaleas from winter damage by creating a nearby wind break with burlap wrapped around stakes.
- Cover hybrid tea roses with styrofoam caps for winter protection, after they have been pruned late in the fall.

When trees and shrubs are planted and pruned correctly, they can become focal points on the lawn, as they do in the Bathurst garden of Brenda and Richard Toth (whose garden is described on page 26).

Kim Hovey, Carlow

Perennials

"Of all the varied objects of creation, there is probably no portion that affords so much gratification and delight to mankind as plants."

Elizabeth Twining, 1868

ardening with perennials is like having lifelong friends. Some of them might only visit me in the early spring and then vanish until the next year; others might make colourful statements for a week or two in the summer before quietly fading into the background. Some produce flowers to keep me company all season long, and others I enjoy spending time with in the fall, when their late blossoms keep life interesting at the end of the growing season. There are even some perennials that make the winter landscape attractive, reminding me that my garden is a year-round venture. And it's hard to pick favourites—though I confess that I'm fond of daylilies and dearly love beebalm and filipendula.

Perennial plants, by definition, are those that survive from year to year in the garden. Some may bloom the first year they're planted, while others may need one season in the ground before they produce flowers. Still other types of perennials need to grow for a few years before they're sufficiently mature to bloom.

However they grow, perennials make up the majority of the plants in my flower beds, because they are so rewarding to garden with. I have some that I grew from seed, some transplanted from the gardens of friends and relatives, some purchased at nurseries, and some that I was given by the gardeners featured in this book. Each plant has a story and holds a memory as I cultivate it throughout the summer.

I've often been asked whether perennials are less expensive to garden with than annuals, and whether or not they are less work. After all, these are plants that keep coming back year after year, unlike annuals, which need to be purchased and planted afresh each June. I usually answer by confessing that neither the cost or the work ends when a garden is planted with perennials. In the first place, perennial plants are so varied that it's hard to restrict yourself to just a few. Like me, most gardeners are fanatical about trying new things, which makes it hard for them to resist placing a yearly order from a seed catalogue or picking up a new species or two every visit to the garden centre. This is the behaviour of an addict, of course, but that is what perennial lovers usually become.

With respect to the work required to grow perennials, there's no such thing as "plant it and leave it." Growing perennials takes lots of effort. There will be the weeding, the staking, and the fertilizing each year. Then there will be the need to deadhead, to divide overgrown plants, to cut back dead foliage at the end of the growing season, and to provide winter protection. Growing perennials successfully also takes lots of planning. Gardeners have to think about a plant's height, spread, flower and foliage colour, and its preference for sun or shady sites, before deciding how and what to plant in a perennial bed. It's also helpful to know a plants' bloom time because a perennial garden is most attractive if there is always something in flower.

Some gardeners use perennials as the framework for their garden, mixing them with colourful annuals, evergreens, and flowering shrubs. They might plant them around their water gardens and complement them with garden sculpture and outdoor art. They might use them to surround a patio, to border a fence, to camouflage a shed, or to climb an arbour. They grow them to attract birds and butterflies to their gardens. There's no limit to the appeal of perennials—especially to the owners of these New Brunswick gardens.

Barbara Telford
Woodsmoke Farm Perennials, Upper Gagetown

Woodsmoke Farm isn't just an ordinary garden. Almost ten years in the making, this beautiful array of hardy perennials is really a demonstration area to highlight plants that owner Barb Telford has to offer her gardening clients. A firm believer in selling what she herself has tried and tested in New Brunswick's harsh climate, Barb has constructed not only a display of plants that have proven to be winter hardy in the province, but has situated the material in and around an attractive water garden, a series of tiered planting beds, a shade house for sun-shy species, and a pond that provides her nursery's irrigation water.

The gardens at Woodsmoke Farm feature ornate wooden arbours to support the growth of grapes, clematis, and honeysuckle. Old-fashioned picket fences serve as backdrops and garden dividers, inviting flagstone paths are surrounded by creeping and woolly thyme, and handmade cedar plaques provide plant names for handy reference. A garden shed sports a roof of carved cedar shakes, while willow furniture offers a resting spot for the weary. The resident donkey, peacocks, and sheep watch from the nearby pasture, and butterfly baths are placed throughout the garden, just waiting for passing flutterers to alight.

Visitors touring the gardens at Woodsmoke Farm are always attracted to the incredible displays of peonies. These specimens grow on a gentle slope at the back of the nursery, which seems to be an almost perfect spot for creating healthy, strong-stemmed plants able to keep erect even when loaded with blossoms. Barb's favourite variety is Felix Krause, a deep red, old-fashioned peony that's a stalwart performer. She loves it so much that she admits to considering the rest of her collection to be "just peonies."

Barbara Telford's garden at Woodsmoke Farm offers a beautiful array of hardy perennials.

Barb says that the secret to success for all peony varieties is to plant them in well-drained, loamy soil, in full sun, and then to "just leave them alone. Peonies hate to be disturbed and will respond to repeated transplanting by refusing to flower." She assures her customers that peonies can grow and bloom happily in the same garden spot for years and years if sited correctly when first planted. She also notes that peonies don't need much fertilizer, except for a bit of compost sprinkled at the base of the plant each spring, and they don't really need to be mulched for winter protection, especially after they get established in a planting location.

In addition to peonies, Woodsmoke Farm has a varied collection of iris. There is a bearded cultivar called Kumquat with gorgeous yellow-orange blooms; another variety is appropriately called Butter Cookie, with flowers that look good enough to eat. Barb recommends that bearded types of iris be planted so that their rhizomes are just at the soil's surface. They do best in well-drained soil, in a sunny spot in the garden, though after several years in one garden location they may start to die back at the centre. This is a sign that the plants need dividing, which isn't difficult. Begin the job, after their blooming period is over, by removing flower stalks and then teasing individual rhizomes away from the perimeter of the clump. These divisions can be regrouped in a new planting spot, or returned to the same location after it has been tilled and mixed with fresh compost.

Newly planted irises will need to be kept well watered until they get established. Winter protection with evergreen boughs, for both newly planted and long standing iris beds, is beneficial.

Siberian Iris and Japanese Iris are also in Barb's collection; these are good for gardeners who are looking for plants that grow best in a wetter environment—near the edge of a pond, for example, or beside a stream or ditch. These types of iris have a fibrous root system and strap-like foliage that stays attractive all summer. They'll only need to be divided if they get too big for their planting area, because they don't tend to die out in the centre like their bearded cousins. But they'll appreciate some fertilizer each spring, either in the form of compost tea or composted manure scratched into the soil where they're planted.

If asked whether or not she has a favourite perennial, Barb replies "rodgersia," without hesitation. These are interesting plants for moist soils in partial shade. If they are planted in full sun, where soil dries out readily, rodgersia will wilt and eventually die. But when planted along ponds or streams, they develop the most luxurious foliage and spikes of fuzzy flowers that "are tropical looking," according to Barb. Rodgersia is hardy to zone 4, and will tolerate most New Brunswick winters, but will benefit from a cover of evergreen boughs for protection from the cold.

Woodsmoke Farm grows many other perennials, including lilies and hosta, astilbe and veronicas, pasque flowers, and an amazing number of daylilies. Barb considers full-sized daylilies to be the ultimate plant for large properties, but she also sells miniature varieties that will fit anywhere. "Daylilies are low-maintenance plants that thrive in a wide variety of soil and moisture conditions."

Gardeners who love "hens and chickens" (*Sempervivens* sp.) should be sure to include a stop at the Woodsmoke Farm's water garden in their tour through the nursery. Tucked into rocky crevices and sprawling out over sandy ledges, these clumps of darling little succulents look like miniature mounds of living stone, in colours of red, green, brown, and grey. These are great perennials for children to grow because no part of them is toxic. Barb proves that they're actually edible plants by popping an offshoot into her mouth. Such eccentricities are just part of her gardening technique, and accompany her habit of relating stories and legends about her plants to visitors at Woodsmoke Farm. "Do you know how Lady's Mantle got its name?" she might ask. But then, to Barb, growing perennials is more than just a business. She considers each and every specimen in her garden to be a kindred spirit. She pampers them all summer and then leaves them to rest all winter under blankets of snow—a great working relationship, don't you think?

Madeline Gibson
St. Stephen

Madeline Gibson is mid-way through her eighth decade of life and still actively gardening at her home in St. Stephen, N.B. She has always been famous for her remarkable perennial garden—adjacent to the main highway entering this border town—but her success with plants goes beyond her outdoor flower and vegetable gardens to her indoor collection of African violets and houseplants. Basically, Madeline just enjoys growing things and readily admits that "gardening keeps me young!"

Her green thumb is something that Madeline has always loved to share. Many years ago, after she got tired of looking over other people's hedges to get a glimpse of their gardens, she decided to open her own garden for public viewing so that people would feel comfortable enough to drop by and take a good look rather than gaze at her garden from the road. She put an attractive sign up near the driveway with big letters spelling

Madeline Gibson opens her St. Stephen garden for public viewing.

"OPEN." Since then, she's had visitors from near and far, some of whom are New Brunswick gardeners, but many of whom are tourists and travellers from far away countries; she has everyone sign her guest book to mark their visit. And every August, during St. Stephen's popular Chocolate Festival she welcomes folks who are brought to her garden by the official Chocolate-Fest Bus on scheduled tours. She answers the many questions that these garden guests have, and she listens to stories and learns new ideas in turn. "I truly enjoy all of these people," she says. "They always have something to share and most of them are really into gardening!"

Madeline begins her gardening year by combing seed catalogues to select interesting annuals and perennials. She starts all of her seeds in her own small greenhouse, and usually has extras, which she saves for the local garden club's spring plant sale.

Some annuals that she has often chosen to add colour and contrast to her perennial collection include portulaca (for the very front of the border to provide splashes of bright pink, yellow, and orange), lavatera (for its striking green foliage and deep, rose-coloured flowers), marigolds (for their cheery yellow and orange blooms) and impatiens (for a shady spot under a flowering crab at the corner of her border). She also loves lemon beebalm, which has attractive pink blossoms and lemon-scented foliage. "It's appropriately named," she says, "because the bees just love it!"

The last several summers have not been kind to the Gibson Garden because of the long periods of drought. She chose not to water her garden during those dry spells because she follows the "wise old gardener's philosophy that says unless you water, water, water, don't bother!" This means that unless sufficient water is applied, on a regular basis, to percolate deep down into the soil, plant roots will tend to remain at the surface, waiting for the little bit of water that comes from the spray of a garden hose, for short durations, every so often. And shallow-rooted plants are stressed plants that don't grow to their potential. On the other hand, when garden plants aren't watered at all, their roots tend to grow deep into the soil, searching out natural water reserves. Deeply-rooted plants are healthier and better able to tolerate drought conditions.

Madeline's favourite perennials are daylilies. She now has 75 different cultivars that range from the traditional orange and yellow flowers to unusual specimens with deep chocolate, intense red, or bicolour flowers. "Daylilies require so little care," she says "and look good even when they're finished blooming." Other perennials in the border include rudbeckias with bronzy orange flowers that add a striking contrast to the shasta daisies and yellow Marguerite. Purple coneflowers blend with rose coloured phlox and pink poppies. She's had lavish displays of delphiniums over the years, but has lost lots of them in recent seasons. "They were old and at the end of their lifespan," she says regretfully, "but I've started more from seed and they'll soon be good and showy." And, because Madeline is concerned about colour for her garden right to the end of the growing season, she includes Helenium, or sneezewort, which doesn't bloom until late summer. It produces small, yellowish brown, daisy-like flowers and grows to an average of 1.25 m on rigid stems that withstand the stresses of wind and rain—a great plant for the back of the border.

There are few weeds in Madeline's garden, and what weeds do grow are removed by hand. She chooses not to use a mulch on her beds, preferring to see well-cultivated earth at the base of her plants. This also allows her to work in fertilizer or compost throughout the growing season, when plants finish blooming. At the beginning of each season, she adds a balanced granular fertilizer (such as 10-10-10) to the soil in her border.

Like all gardeners, Madeline has to put up with insect problems. She starts by removing spent flower blossoms and any dead leaves on a daily basis. She feels that this routine husbandry along with good, fertile soil keeps plants healthy, and healthy plants don't attract insects as much as unhealthy plants. If she does have an outbreak of bugs, she sprays with a homemade, environmentally-friendly pesticide consisting of half a cup of hot pepper flakes, six tablespoons of detergent (either liquid or powdered), and one gallon of water. "It works marvellously against aphids," she explains, "and it will not burn a plant's leaves."

At the end of each growing season, Madeline cuts back the stems of her perennial plants to ground level to prepare her border for overwintering. She doesn't do much in the way of cold-weather protection, preferring to allow plants to cope with the winter conditions. Over the years, she has lost some iris because of this, but these have been replaced with more winter-hardy daylilies.

Madeline's legendary green thumb must be a family trait because her daughter, Mary Louise Peters, is now an active gardener. Mary Louise also lives in St. Stephen, so mother and daughter share plants back and forth, and enjoy each other's company on trips to gardens and garden centres around New Brunswick. Gardening is definitely a family activity for these Gibson gals.

Judy and Bill Whalen
Quispamsis

On a hillside lot overlooking the beautiful Kennebecasis River, Judy and Bill Whalen have created a garden that's a product of their love of nature and their desire to produce a healthy lifestyle for themselves and their family. For the past twenty-five years, they've been sculpturing their landscape and renovating the contours of their property to produce a green space that provides them with a cottage garden setting. Their labours have been arduous at times, but the results are really outstanding.

Back in the early 70s, when the Whalens decided to take on the challenge of purchasing a house built in 1917, they were determined to have a garden where they could grow most of their own food organically, and an area where they could keep bees, chickens, and rabbits. They also considered the importance of beauty in their surroundings and planned to site flower beds, shrubs, and trees so that these could be viewed not only from the grounds but also from various windows in the house.

The changes to their landscape began when the Whalens planted a cedar hedge along the entire eastern length of the property. They chose to do this because it was obvious that their river-side location was subject to strong, gusting winds at all times of the year. They were sure that the hedge would create a microclimate to allow some protection from those strong breezes—and they were right. Today that hedge is fourteen feet

"A passion for perennials," says Judy Whalen, "quickly becomes an addiction."

high, and so thick that it's difficult to see through. Not only does it provide protection from the wind, but it has created a private oasis around the entire Whalen garden. You'd never know that they were surrounded by an ever-increasing number of new homes and subdivisions in this popular area near the Gondola Point ferry.

After the hedge was planted, Judy and Bill started to develop a planting scheme for the rest of their property. They had to consider the slope of the land and a stream that ran through the centre of their backyard. They had to work around the chicken coop and storage barn, the beehives and the rabbit hutch, and they had to keep in mind where there was shade and where there was sun. Before actually planting anything they took lots of time to prepare the soil, because a good garden "starts from the ground up," says Judy. They added manure from their hens and worked in their own compost; "home gardeners," says Bill, "should have a compost pile going at all times." Compost is a great source of organic matter, the backbone of a healthy soil.

One of their first planting projects involved the construction of a lath house, under which they planted a collection of fiddlehead ferns. Those ferns have grown and multiplied significantly over the ensuing years, and now provide the Whalens with enough fiddleheads each spring to pick and freeze for a whole year's supply. Honeysuckle vines were planted at the base of the posts that support this lath house, as were Minnesota and Beta grapes, from which Judy makes jelly each summer.

The Whalens first perennials and shrubs came from family and friends. All of these plants were special, but it soon became obvious that the couple had definite preferences, and they divided up the gardening chores so that Bill planted what he liked, and Judy did the same. "I'm not as flowery as Judy is," admits Bill, "so I do the trees and shrubs, and she does the perennials and annuals." From tree seeds collected during some of his travels across the country, he has been able to grow some interesting and unusual specimens in his New Brunswick home. He enjoys the challenge of determining seed germination requirements and hardiness levels for different woody species.

Judy, meanwhile, is passionate about perennials. "There is so much colour when they're in bloom," she remarks, "and they're so big, so robust…so outstanding!" She says that "a passion for perennials quickly becomes an addiction, and then you become a collector!" But when asked to decide what perennial is her favourite, Judy has to admit that her likes and dislikes change. She is especially fond of helenium because it makes the fall garden so colourful. But she consistently favours rudbeckia and tall phlox too. An avid photographer, she has taken hundreds of pictures of these three types of perennials.

And the Whalen perennial collection is vast. As their garden plan developed over the years, they integrated daylilies, evening primroses, delphiniums, foxglove, the peonies that had been planted by the previous owners of the house, sedum, and dozens of other species, many of which they grew from seed in their own small greenhouse. The Whalens purposely combined perennials with annuals, vegetables, and herbs. They left seedlings of self-sown poppies and sunflowers where they came up between the tomatoes and carrots. They placed flowering shrubs next to the raspberry patch. They moved plants around the garden routinely, mixing and matching foliage and flower colours in pleasing combinations.

Although busiest with their gardening tasks in the spring—when vegetables have to be planted, when shrubs have to be pruned, and when their perennials have to be divided or moved—Judy and Bill note that "there is important gardening to be done in the fall," especially with respect to adding nutrients to the soil. They have recently begun using crab and lobster meal (a good, organic source of nitrogen) as a fall fertilizer around the base of their woody plants. They have also worked it into the soil in new planting areas that they're preparing for the next spring.

Some years, when time allows, the Whalens cut back their perennials to ground level after the plants' foliage has been hit by autumn frost. But in other years (either because they're off on a holiday, visiting relatives, or otherwise occupied) they leave this type of garden maintenance until spring. "The skeletons of perennials, sticking up through the snow, make great photographs in the winter," says Bill, proving that the Whalens enjoy their garden all year long.

Reno and Beatrice Long
Grand Falls

On a quiet corner lot in the town of Grand Falls, New Brunswick, Reno and Beatrice Long enjoy watching their garden move through its annual progression of colour from spring until fall. The couple live in a charming house built in the mid 1800s. It's bordered on two sides by an expertly-clipped cedar hedge, and is surrounded by mature trees. The hedge and trees provide a natural way to cope with the heat from intense summer sun, but

Although limited by shade, Beatrice and Reno Long have been able to grow a surprising variety of perennials.

these permanent landscape features also pose a great gardening dilemma. "We are limited by our shade," says Beatrice, when describing the challenges they've had in establishing the many flower beds that grace their property. After all, low light conditions aren't appropriate for many types of perennials. But the Longs have been able to grow a surprising variety and have succeeded in always having something in bloom.

Spring in the Long's garden begins with bulbs. They have tulips, daffodils, grape hyacinth, and ornamental onions that produce dainty yellow blossoms. Beatrice notes that they have never had trouble with squirrels digging up their bulbs, and it might just be because these pesky critters don't like the smell of these alliums, which are strong-scented cousins to the vegetable garden onion. The Longs also have crocus coming up all over the lawn just after the snow melts each year. Gardeners who try to naturalize bulbs this way have to make sure not to mow the grass around them until their foliage has turned completely yellow. Otherwise, the plants eventually loose their vigour and die out. But Bernice says that their lawn is slow to grow anyway each spring, so they have always have a crocus success story.

After their bulbs have run their course, the Longs enjoy a succession of blooms from their many perennials in various beds around the house: pansies, poppies, astilbe, beebalm, lilies, iris, daisies, daylilies, balloon-flowers, hosta, and peonies. There are also herbs like lavender, lemon thyme, and feverfew. And there are shrub roses from the explorer series, namely David Thompson, Martin Frobisher, John Cabot, and Therese Bugnet. "Leo is the rose grower," says Bea, who prefers herbaceous plants and has been expanding her growing area in the last few years. She starts her beds by defining the outline on the ground (in one case she laid a cloth bed sheet down on the grass to make the outline for a rectangular bed). After removing the sod from the ground, she prepares the soil for planting by mixing in a bit of peat moss and some compost from her compost bin. Her most recent project has been the creation of a permanent border running along the edge of the lawn. It contains plants that she has "rescued" from friends' gardens…species like stachys, yarrow, delphinium, monkshood, and perennial sunflowers. The border is designed with different foliage colours, different bloom colours, and different plant heights in an appealing combination. It's backed by a hedge of Annabelle hydrangea, which the Longs keep under control by pruning it back, each fall, to six or eight inches above ground level.

Although perennials are the most prominent plants in this landscape, there are a couple of annuals worthy of note. In a bed along the foundation of the house, Bea always plants pink-flowered geraniums. She's had these plants for twenty years and keeps them over the winter on a sunny window ledge in the living room. The other "fun" plants that she and Leo enjoy growing each summer are morning glories; they start these in a large planter pot each spring and train them up a trellis all season. The plants are covered with sky-blue blossoms that keep appearing until the first frost causes them to wither and die, and are real eye catchers at the side of the carport.

Bea has passed her love of gardening to some of her students at the John Caldwell School in Grand Falls, where she and fellow teachers have supervised the planting of perennials, shrubs and trees by children of all ages from kindergarten to grade 12. She has also been actively involved in beautification programs throughout the community including planting projects along the town's main boulevard and in the park around the massive waterfalls on the Saint John River that give this municipality its name. For Bea, gardening is not only a favourite hobby, but also part of an intimate connection with other citizens in her part of New Brunswick.

Brenda and Richard Toth
Bathurst

When Brenda and Richard Toth moved into their house twenty years ago, their backyard was really just a big depression in the ground. The area was full of natural springs and boulders and was anything but level. "We faced some real challenges," says Richard. But that didn't stop the couple from proceeding with their plans for a garden. They lugged away rocks and brought in loads of topsoil. They built a large retaining wall, directly behind the house, to deal with the steep grade into the back of the property. At the bottom of this retaining wall they created a streambed to channel water from one side of their lot to the other, and then sculptured the rest of the area to blend in with existing topography. All of this took many gardening seasons to complete, but now Brenda and Richard can sit on their back deck and look down into their delightful sunken garden.

One eye-catching feature of the garden is the cotoneaster hedge on either side of a bricked walking path, started with cuttings from Richard's mother's garden in Alberta. Cotoneaster has shiny green leaves and produces attractive black berries late in the summer. It's a terrific hedge plant and has been surprisingly hardy in this zone 3 garden. Huge clumps of hosta grow beside the hedge and seem perfectly happy in a spot that gets sun all day. Gardeners often restrict their planting of hosta to shadier sites, but certain varieties will do extremely well in brighter conditions.

The stream that was a challenge during the original landscaping of the property is another striking feature of the Toth's garden. Richard built a footbridge over the stream, lining its edges with stone and planting water-loving plants like yellow-flag iris on its banks.

Just beyond the hedge, an attractive sundial rests on a concrete pedestal. A rock garden has perennials flowering at various times through the summer, giving a show of yellow, then blue, then white. The rock garden tumbles in curved beds on either side of two stone steps. There are daylilies and artemesia, old-fashioned bleeding hearts and shasta daisies, lamb's ears and beebalm as tall backdrop plants. In front of these are lower-growing autumn joy sedum, ground phlox, and succulent stonecrop planted around clusters of rocks. Annuals like lavatera, sunflowers, celosia, and dusty miller are thrown in each year for good measure. Quaint rabbits, chickens, and sheep (molded in

The Toths built a footbridge over their stream, lining its edges with stone and planting water-loving plants like yellow-flag iris.

concrete and painted by Brenda) add their own special charm, peering out from around the blossoms.

Beside the rock garden is the couple's vegetable garden where Brenda plants cucumbers in wire tomato cages, to keep them from sprawling all over the adjacent onions and carrots. There are also tomatoes and beans, but these are interspersed with bedding plants and daylilies "just for colour."

Brenda is an addict of herbaceous perennial but is especially fond of bearded iris. She considers these plants to be real heartbreakers, however, "because you only have two weeks to enjoy their blooms each summer" before they fade away. She finds iris to be heavy feeders so waters them with a fertilizer solution of 15-30-15 at least twice in the summer. She also uses compost and manure in her planting beds, or scratches in 6-12-12 if she can't get enough compost from her bins.

Richard is the keeper of the compost. He constructed a compost unit at the back of the garden, tucked neatly in a corner under some trees. It's surrounded with some of his unique sculpture, including a life-sized "man of steel" and a decorative iron plate (really a remodeled electrical panel). "There's more to this garden than plants," says Richard, who is an accomplished painter as well as a sculptor. Also contributing to the garden is the recent addition of a cedar fence at the back of the property, which took Richard most of one entire summer to construct. It's rustic appearance is a beautiful backdrop for some new perennial beds that Brenda has created. He's told her that one side of the fence can be hers and the other is off limits, as far as new garden space is concerned. It's to remain unobstructed by plants, he insists. Brenda and Richard often joke like that about the garden. She isn't comfortable letting him weed, for example, because "who knows what he would take out with them!" But then there aren't many weeds anyway, says Richard because "they don't even dare to come up when she's around." Between the two of them, they manage to keep their garden immaculate and they eventually agree on what can be planted where. He admits to not having a flair for design, and she confesses that her success is just serendipitous. Whatever the case, the Toths make great gardening partners and they have created a wonderful garden and outdoor art gallery.

Kim Hovey
Carlow

Several years ago, when she'd had enough of looking out her kitchen window at wild raspberry canes and burdocks, Kim Hovey decided that the time had come to tackle the weedy jungle around her home overlooking the Shikatehawk Stream, near Lockhart's Mill, New Brunswick. She had already been gardening for some time, but had always wanted a garden for lilies and daylilies, and it seemed like the right time and place to build one.

Kim's project started with the help of a front-end loader. Because she wanted a sloped garden on both sides of an entrance into the basement of the house, she needed a heavy machine to dig out and taper the site before she could begin planting. She also wanted the area at the base of the slope to be wide and gravelled to provide easy access from the house to the bank of the Shikatehawk and the nearby highway.

Kim designed her lily garden as a series of wooden cribs, terraced along the slope, with steps running up the centre to lawn areas above. The basic earth work was completed late one fall, and the job of readying the cribs for planting started the next spring. She mixed peat moss into imported loam, adding a bit of vermiculite (for drainage) before loading it into the cribs. The filled cribs were narrow enough so that she could work at planting and weeding without ever having to step on the soil surface. "That way the soil never gets compacted." Compacted soil is hard for plant roots to penetrate, which leads to poor growth and plant stress.

After the soil was ready, Kim began planting many varieties of daylily roots, ordered from nurseries in Ontario and Quebec. She also divided a large number of daylilies from plants that were growing elsewhere in her garden and moved them into the new cribbed beds. Kim used her own preferred planting technique for making sure that the daylily's roots were properly covered. "I dig a hole that's twice the diameter of the daylily's root system," she explains, "and then I make a mound in the centre of the hole's bottom." Over this mound she fans out the daylily's roots, so all are directed downward into the base of the hole and the crown of the plant is directly over the centre of the top of the mound. "I find that when you just make a depression in the ground, without the mound in the middle, the daylily roots tend to get pointed upward a bit when the soil is put back in around them," she notes. And that sets the plants back, she has found.

But before Kim replaces the soil in her planting hole, she dusts a bit of bonemeal over the daylily roots. She then covers them with soil, but only so that the hole is half filled. "I add some water," Kim says, "so that it gets to the roots right away." After the water has soaked in completely, she puts the rest of the soil in the hole and tamps it in place. Then she mulches the entire bed with a four-inch (ten cm) layer of shredded bark to keep in moisture and keep out weeds. She makes sure to remove blooms from the plants as soon as they are formed during a plant's first growing year, but after that, her daylilies are allowed to bloom. At the end of the growing season she cuts the plants' foliage back to ground level, but finds she doesn't have to provide them with any winter protection. "Daylilies are tough, and they cope with New Brunswick winters very well. You can transplant them anytime in the summer or even move them several times in one season and they'll still be OK." But that's not the only reason that Kim loves daylilies. "They're called a 'Devotion Plant,'" she says. "I'm devoted to them and they're devoted to me!"

While planting daylilies, Kim prepared her beds for lilies. She'd ordered a wide variety of asiatic lilies, oriental lilies, and regals, paying close attention to each type's bloom time and final height. Because lily bulbs usually arrive from mail order nurseries in late fall, she had to do some ground work in the beds to prepare for their delivery date, because the soil would be too frozen to work with if she waited until the bulbs arrived before digging. And she recommends her method to everyone who plants lilies.

"I dig the planting holes in the garden," she explains, "and keep the soil removed in a place where it won't freeze." She then stuffs the holes full of newspaper to keep their sides from collapsing during autumn rains. When the bulbs are finally delivered, she stores them in her unheated garage overnight to give them a chill, then puts them outside in a box for the next night so they get even more used to the cold. Finally, on the following day, she sets each bulb in its pre-dug planting hole, along with bone meal and some fine sawdust. "I put the soil back on top of them, but I don't add water because the ground around the base of the bulb is usually so frozen that it wouldn't allow water to percolate away from the bulb" (the water would end up as a frozen mass around the lily, which isn't the best thing to have happen). If bulbs are small, she mulches them with evergreen boughs, but if they're large, she finds that they overwinter well, with no added protection.

Kim staked her lilies in their first growing season, because they were single stalks and prone to breaking off in the wind. But in the summers that followed, she found that her lilies tend to send up multiple stems that have enough strength to stand upright by themselves. "If I was growing them in a windy spot, it might be a different story," she says, but her new cribbed garden is in a sheltered location, so she hasn't had to worry about damaging gusts.

It has been five years since Kim began the lily and daylily project, and she's still working at getting it just right. "Last year I watched to see what colour blossoms were next to each other and when they came into flower." She marked the ones that she plans to move, either because their colours clash badly with their neighbour, or because a cluster of plants bloomed all at the same time, leaving a void when they were finished. And Kim wants to make sure that the more robust growers are placed behind shorter varieties, rather than in front. It will be a summer-long project, but you can imagine the end result!

Murray Alexander
Welshpool

As was the case in most parts of eastern Canada, the drought of the summer of 1999 was hard on Murray Alexander's garden. And even though his six-acre property is bordered by water, it's the salt water of the Bay of Fundy—not much help for parched earth. But that didn't stop this quiet, gentle man from getting enjoyment from being out of doors, tending to his per-

Murray Alexander uses colour in pleasing combinations.

ennial beds, shrubs, and vegetable garden. His island landscape has been in the family for a long time and he continues to care for plants that have been growing in the same spot for many years, dry weather or not.

Most notable in his collection are some yellow-flowered daylilies that highlight the centre of a perennial bed near the edge of his lawn. They grow so vigorously that he's had to divide them from time to time with an axe. They also have "flowers so big that a hummingbird can sit inside the blossom," he says, with obvious pride. Accompanying these daylilies are white and pink astilbe, Asiatic lilies, silver mound artemesia, liatris, and a number of intensely blue-flowered monkshood.

In a narrow bed beside his garage, Murray has created a miniature hedge of candytuft against the base of the building. This low-growing perennial is completely covered with tiny white flowers each spring and maintains a fresh green look all summer, especially if dead flowers are removed at the end of the bloom period. These candytuft replaced a bed of tall phlox whose foliage had been infected with powdery mildew so often that the plants deteriorated, and were eventually removed. Powdery mildew is a fungal disease that is often a problem for phlox, especially if plants are overcrowded. Good air circulation through and around the perimeter of each plant is helpful to combat infestation, and so is planting some of the modern, mildew-resistant varieties now available at garden centres.

Murray uses colour in pleasing combinations. In a small rockery, beside the front steps of his cottage, he has grouped a cream-coloured astilbe with the attractive foliage of a variegated hosta, the reddish hues of stonecrop sedum, and the pink flowers of chives. Gray stones and rust-red bricks accent the plants.

Murray also likes to have flowering shrubs in the landscape; he grows lilacs and roses, but his favourite is a beauty bush (*Kolkwitzia amabilis*) which "leafs out very late in the spring," making it hard to tell whether or not it has survived the winter. The bush produces pale pink flowers in early June and foliage that turns reddish in fall, making it a fine specimen plant.

One unusual perennial—an Egyptian onion—grows in Murray's vegetable patch. These intriguing plants taste like onions and are completely edible, but don't "act" like onions because they develop daughter bulbs at the top of their leaves instead of at the base. Sometimes called "walking onions," the plants' leaves collapse to the ground in the fall after they've been hit by frost; in this way, daughter bulbs come in contact with the soil, where they overwinter with great success. And they'll start growing again the next spring, right where they planted themselves, usually some distance away from the original parent plant. Over the years, these plants can travel quite a distance if left to their own devices—hence the name "walking onion"! Murray keeps a collection of them at the end of his rhubarb patch, where they seem completely under control, just like the rest of this neat and tidy garden.

Diane Richard
Grand Falls

When Diane Richard moved into her new home in Grand Falls a few years ago, she was given a housewarming party by her friends. "Everybody brought a plant from their own garden as a gift" she says, "and it was so appropriate because I was just beginning the landscaping." All of those plants went into her "friendship garden," where they are a treasured reminder of the generosity of her fellow gardeners. And from those first plants, Diane proceeded to transform her entire property into an award-winning garden. In conjunction with a Communities in Bloom competition in the summer of 1998, judges found her efforts to be worth first place in the town's home garden category. It's not difficult to see why. "It's my passion and my obsession," she admits. From her first moments of digging in the earth, "I was captivated with gardening."

On the street side of the house, Diane placed a wide, interlocking brick walkway to lead from the driveway to the front door. Between the walkway and the garage wall is a raised planter bed made from stone in which she has placed low-growing perennials, a climbing rose, and some licorice plant (an annual with soft grey foliage that trails over the planter's edge). The opposite side of the walkway is bordered by a bed full of shrubs and perennials. It's outer edge has been sculpted to match the curves of the walkway and its surface has been mulched with barkchips. The yellow hues of variegated hosta and gold-leaf spirea, the dark wine shade of purple-leafed sandcherry and Little Princess spirea flowers, the grey-green of creeping juniper, and the creamy blossoms of a peegee hydrangea create a colour scheme that complements the grey and white siding of her house.

Along the sides of the house, where a grassy strip provides a pathway to the back garden, Diane placed a trough of crushed rock to keep the area between the lawn and the foundation of the house tidy and easy to care for. (The trough is only 25 cm wide but has helped to eliminate the problem of having to use hand clippers or an electric snipper where the lawnmower is unable to

Diane Richard keeps feeders and baths full so that birds stay close by. If these are filled sporadically, birds will migrate to other feeding stations.

get close to the house.) The trough is separated from the lawn by a rubber edging, which keeps grass roots from invading it.

Walking into Diane's backyard is like walking into a private oasis: there are pockets of gardens over the whole area, stretching from the house to the back edge of the property. And at the end of the garden is a breathtaking view—an uninterrupted line of sight over the Saint John River, just where it approaches the famous Grand Falls. The scene is framed by giant pine and spruce trees, and makes a spectacular backdrop for a garden.

Keeping birds and butterflies in mind, Diane has also established a number of feeding stations in the garden and an ornate, pedestaled bird bath. She keeps the feeders and the bath full so that birds stay close by. When a gardener only remember to fill feeders sporadically, birds tend to migrate to other, more consistantly-attended feeding stations. Once you start feeding birds, its important to be dedicated to the task.

The back of Diane's house has a comfortable deck and patio from which she can look out over her beautiful garden and on to the view of the river in the distance. The resident birds and butterflies give her as much pleasure as her plants do. But her plans for the yard aren't finished yet. She points to an expanse of grass, at the side of the backyard and describes her next garden project. "There will be a miniature footbridge in that place next year," she describes. "I plan to have it stretch over a dry pond lined with stone." No doubt it will be surrounded by an additional collection of shrubs and flowers, but the plan is still evolving. "This garden just keeps on expanding" she admits. What gardener would find a problem with that?

Deanna Baldwin
Welshpool

When Deanna and Leo Baldwin moved back to Campobello several years ago, they purchased a property just over an acre in size and derelict for some time. Its house had been built in 1862, which meant it had to be gutted inside to make it livable. This would be a long-term project, one that would take up most of their time and energy over the next few years. But that didn't mean Deanna was content to avoid the landscaping. "When we came here, there was a mock orange bush, some daylilies and some sedum creeping all over the place," she says. But she could imagine how the property—which looks out over the channel separating Campobello from Maine—could be transformed into a series of terraced gardens, connected by gravelled paths.

But as is the case over much of the island, Deanna's gardening plans had to work around one factor of island living. She'd have to keep in mind that bedrock was just below the surface on every inch of the property. "I knew that I was going to be working with a thousand-year-old ledge," she admits, "and I knew that it might take me years and years to make the garden I wanted." But she was determined to get started, and today, almost a decade after beginning the process of reclaiming an overgrown landscape, she's well on her way to the garden of her dreams.

One of Deanna's first projects was her herb garden. She laid it out in a flat area at the back of the property, adjacent to a line of mature spruce trees that borders the street. She made a circular bed and edged it with red bricks, placed flat in the ground side by side. She then ran brick paths across the diameter of the circle, so that they crossed in the centre, dividing the bed into four wedge-shaped sections. Within these sections she planted perennial herbs of all types, including species of thyme, silver king artemesia, silver mound, sea thrift (*Armeria maritimea*), oregano, sage, tarragon, and chives. She also added annual herbs like basil and parsley at the beginning of the planting season. The soil here was sandy and well drained, which was perfect for herbs, but also a great place for ants. In fact, each brick seemed to have its own colony underneath. "It was as if I'd built them a big condominium," she laughs. After trying all the tricks that people recommend for getting rid of the pesky insects, she's had limited success. She used borax and ant traps. She was told to fill a narrow-necked bottle with sugar water and lay it on its side so that the ants would go in for a drink and drown. Hundreds of them were in the bottle each day, but there were always enough that survived to keep the population expanding in her garden. She even followed one recommendation to take a shovel full from one ant colony and add it to another colony elsewhere in the garden. The idea was that the two populations of ants would battle each other to the death, thus eliminating her problem. "But I think they decided to make love, not war," she chuckles, "because the process didn't seem to make even a tiny dent in the ant numbers in the garden." She's thinking about taking up the bricks around her herbs, to see if that will help, but at present the ants are still thriving in the Baldwin landscape.

After her herb garden, Deanna decided to create a number of perennial beds. She added daylilies to clusters of lupins that grew naturally near the herb garden, and made a garden on top of a large heap of boulders near the driveway. "They were here when we came, and it seemed easier to make a garden out of them than to try to move them." It became her "yellow" garden, where she planted early, spring-blooming perennial alyssum, yellow loosestrife, yellow flowered sedum, yellow and orange gaillardia, and a few yellow marigolds.

Deanna also made a "seaside theme" garden, designed around a few beach finds such as driftwood, seashells, a lobster trap, and buoys. Amongst these marine artifacts she transplanted beach roses, salt grass, beach pea, and sandwort from the nearby shore. Found growing all over the island, she wanted to move their natural beauty into her own garden. And she mulched the whole bed with sand. "I get fresh beach sand each spring to sprinkle over the garden's surface, just to keep it looking like the natural habitat."

At the front of the house, Deanna created a rose garden around an outcropping of ledge. She planted rugosa roses and pavement roses, both of which do well in poor soil, and both of which will bloom all summer with fragrant flowers. "I'm pleased with how well they've survived, even in the shallow soil," Deanna enthuses. She gives them a bit of help with an annual compost application and some granular rose food each spring. She has

Deanna Baldwin grows plants that will survive Campobello's climate without winter protection: "I'm finally realizing just what does well here."

also planted two roses especially for her grandsons. One is a Therese Bugnet, which has relatively thornless deep-red branches that seldom need pruning. The other is an F. J. Grootendorst, commonly referred to as "the carnation of roses" because each bloom has the fringed petals and small double flowers that re-

Perennials

semble carnations. The Grootendorst also has great disease resistance and is tolerant of poor, salty soil…just perfect for Deanna's garden.

To accompany her roses, Deanna has planted mounds of lemon thyme. "I saw the same combination at Kingsbrae Garden in St. Andrews," she recalls, "and it made for a wonderfully attractive combination." The thyme acts as a mulch at the base of the roses, keeping the shallow soil there from eroding when heavy rain hits the bed. The thyme also remains a lush green, even in the drought of the summer.

At the base of the rose bed, where the Baldwin property moves into a densely wooded slope, Deanna created a bark pathway that winds from one side of the rock ledge to the other. She has marked the edge of the pathway with interesting rocks and has built a set of stone steps down to it, through a break in the ledge. The whole area is planted with sedum, snow-in-summer (*Cerastium tomentosum*), hens-and-chicks, creeping jenny, and mother-of-thyme. "I have selected rock garden types of plants for planting in this area," she describes, "because they have to be able to take the drought and the heat."

At the far side of the rose garden, Deanna has been working on her "Millennium Project": a white garden, with every leaf or blossom a white or silver colour. She has planted white-flowered roses (Hendry Hudson and Blanc Double De Coubert), white astilbe, artemesia, daisies, hosta, and "everything else, including annuals, that's some sort of white." It's all to be completed before 2001. She put spring flowering bulbs in her white garden in the fall of 1999, including crocus, daffodils, and tulips. She always plants bulbs in "bulb baskets" and swears by the results. "In the spring, the bulbs come up in attractive clumps," she says, "instead of being spread out singly all over the garden, where they make less of a show of colour." The ten-centimetre-high bulb baskets, which are made of sturdy plastic, are also helpful for avoiding the usual problem of having to wait long enough for the bulbs to die back naturally in the garden before they can be removed or before their foliage is cut back. "After my bulbs are finished blooming, I just dig up the entire basket and set it behind my compost pile, where I cover it over lightly with soil," describes Deanna. That way bulbs can keep on growing until they've built up reserves for the next year. In late summer, she digs the baskets out from their soil covering, takes out any bulbs that might be rotted or damaged, and then replants in the garden.

Deanna doesn't cover anything in her garden at the end of the season, because she wants to grow plants that will survive in a Campobello climate without winter protection. "It's taken me a bit of time, but I'm finally realizing just what does well here," she admits. Those are the plants that she'll continue to keep in her garden.

The Secrets of Gardening with Perennials

- Be sure to prepare the soil in an area that is destined for perennials, because the plants will be growing in it for a long time.
- Learn about the growing requirements for a plant before placing it in the garden, so that you can match preferred soil type, winter hardiness, moisture level and light requirements with the right species.
- Create the outline of a new perennial bed by laying a sheet on the ground and cutting around its edge, or by laying down a garden hose and moving it until you have the desired shape.
- Plant a selection of perennials so that you will always have something in bloom.
- Consider planting flowering shrubs, evergreens, and roses with your perennials, to add contrast in height and form.
- Avoid walking over the surface of the planting bed so that soil doesn't get compacted.
- If you plan to water your perennials, make sure they get a deep watering once a week rather than a shallow watering every day.
- Stake tall growing plants at the very beginning of the season, to keep them from blowing over in the wind.

- Mulch perennial beds to keep down weeds and to retain soil moisture.
- Deadhead perennials at the end of their blooming period, unless you are interested in saving the seeds they might produce.
- Over the winter, cover tender perennials with evergreen boughs.
- When perennials need dividing, share them with friends and neighbours so they'll have a reminder of you in their gardens!

A Trio of Sturdy Perennials

Hosta

There are few herbaceous perennials that can be considered multipurpose. In fact, it's seldom that one can classify more than a handful of species as low maintenance, easily propagated, suitable for various soil types, happy in sun or shade, lovely to look at, and completely winter hardy. Hostas fit the bill. These bold and beautiful foliage plants are tough, versatile, and adaptable. They make for an excellent groundcover that can choke out weeds and blanket a planting area with green from spring until fall. Although hostas have always been known as the mainstay of the shade garden, new sun-tolerant hybrids are being released by plant breeders every year, and there are now varieties of these handsome perennials for just about any spot in the garden.

Hosta—also known as plantain lily or funkia—is native to Japan, China, and Korea, where it grows in moist woodlands and open grasslands. Several species of these serviceable garden plants have been in cultivation for hundreds of years, and there are dozens and dozens of hybrids. Actually, there are now so many hosta varieties with uncertain parentage that they're not even listed with a species name, but simply known by their cultivar name; hosta classification can be confusing.

Hosta fortunei, or the fortune's hosta, has elongated, heart-shaped leaves that are green to grey-green with long, deeply-furrowed leaf stalks. Hybrids of this hosta include Gold Standard, with light gold leaves edged in green; Gloriosa, with green, oval-shaped leaves with white margins; and Aureo-maculata, with yellow-green margins along its yellow leaves. All these hostas have pale lilac flowers and prefer to grow in partial to dense shade. *Hosta plantaginea*, or the August lily hosta, is a fragrant species with large, broad, heart-shaped, glossy green leaves and sparkling white flowers; hybrids of this species have been given variety names such as Aphrodite, Honeybells, and Royal Standard. *Hosta sieboldii* is the seersucker hosta. Its leaves are long and pointed with white edges, and its most famous hybrid is Frances Williams. And then there are hosta species with wavy leaves and with lance-shaped leaves. There are hostas with leaves the size of dinner plates and dwarf varieties that have leaves no bigger than an inch. They all offer an unmatched range of leaf patterns, colours, and sizes. Look for names such as Francee for sun tolerance, Sum and Substance for built-in slug resistance, Elegans for sun or shade, and Ginko Craig for rock gardens.

Hostas are slow growers, so it's tempting to plant them close together when first placing them in the garden. But in the three to four seasons it takes them to reach full size, they can become three times as wide as they are tall, so they should be spaced accordingly from the start. Hostas are one of the last perennials to poke their way through the ground each spring, especially when planted in deep shade; it's best to mark their planting spot, so that plants aren't disturbed by mistake during early-season soil cultivation. Generally speaking, most species and hybrids of hostas perform best in rich, well-drained soil, although species with thick, waxy leaves are better adapted to dry soil conditions than the thin-leaved types. Hostas with dark green or blue-green leaves are the most shade tolerant, while species with yellowish-green leaves are well suited for sunny sites.

Hostas will continue to grow vigorously for years if treated to an annual application of composted manure, and plants will produce more leaf growth if flowers are removed when they finish their blooming period. Hostas respond well to a thick mulch. Not only does a layer of shredded bark or pine needles keep the roots of the plant evenly moist, but it prevents the plant's foliage from being splashed with mud during rainy weather. Finally, to keep slugs from overtaking hostas, surround plants with a thick ring of diatomaceous earth (sold at garden centres as "Fossil Flower") or crushed egg shells, or set out slug bait on a routine basis.

Hollyhock

Hollyhocks have been beloved by generations of gardeners. Tall and graceful, these spectacular biennials have always been splendid feature plants in either a formal or cottage garden setting.

Hollyhocks are one of the oldest plants in cultivation. Native to China, they were first admired by European visitors in the sixteenth century. Those early plant explorers must have been initially impressed with the eight- to ten-foot flower spikes typical of a blooming hollyhock. Later, they learned of the plant's valuable medicinal qualities. The Chinese were aware that the mucilage and oils abundant in hollyhocks were excellent for treating inflammation of the mucous membranes, cough, asthma, chronic gastritis, enteritis, and constipation. That's why the plant's botanic name, Althaea rosea, is so appropriate: it comes from the Greek word "althein," which means "to heal." Even the derivation of the common name hollyhock was probably a clue to the plant's value in days gone by. "Holly" probably refers to the holy reverence given to the plant, and "hoc" comes from the Anglo-Saxon word for mallow. Hollyhocks are members of the Mallow family of plants, the Malvaceae. Hence "hollyhocks"...the blessed mallow.

After hollyhocks were introduced to Europe, their popularity grew immensely. Every herbalist planted hollyhocks for their medicinal value. Walled gardens were soon brightened by stately spires of white, pink, and red flowers. Fences and rock walls, cottage doorways, and borders were always enhanced with hollyhocks. And because these plants seed themselves readily, once a garden had these showy plants, there was little worry they'd ever be absent. In fact, in the British Isles, hollyhocks are often found growing wild on waste ground that was once a garden, or in areas where they've escaped from cultivation. In the present day Balkans, selected cultivars of hollyhocks are grown as field crops for the pharmaceutical industry; extracts of the plant are used in preparations for skin disorders and other ailments.

The first hollyhocks brought to Europe (and their cousins that accompanied early colonists to North America) produced single blossoms that could be as large as three inches in diameter. These types of hollyhocks were truly biennial and would not bloom until their second summer of growth. Modern plant breeders have produced new hollyhock cultivars with both single and double flowers that have various petal forms: some fluted, some lobed, some resembling a powder puff. And the colours are amazing—rose, white, yellow, dark maroon—every shade but blue. Most newer breeds of hollyhocks will bloom the year they're planted from seed, and are somewhat shorter than their old-fashioned counterparts.

Hollyhocks grow well in many types of soil, but are never happy if their root systems are always wet, so good drainage is essential. They need full sun, and prefer uncrowded conditions with plenty of air circulation; they are susceptible to infections of rust and mildew, both fungal diseases perpetuated by excess moisture on foliage. Mature plants will bloom from July to September each year, with flower buds opening from the base of the stalk first.

These plants are most suitable for the back of perennial borders and in garden spots sheltered from high winds. Because of their height and heavy flower stalks, they're prone to toppling over, especially when nearly ready to bloom, so they'll probably need to be staked or supported against a fence or wall.

Seeds of hollyhocks should be sown directly in the garden in early spring. If seedling plants are purchased at a nursery or transplanted from a friend's garden, they should be handled carefully as roots are large and brittle. Once plants reach blooming size, seed capsules should be allowed to mature on the plant so they can eventually spew their contents over the surrounding garden. Then you'll have hollyhocks year after year and be able to enjoy their impressive blooms as gardeners have for centuries.

Loosestrife

Most Canadian gardeners are aware of the concerns that environmentalists have about growing loosestrife in a garden—the purple loosestrife known to some as the "magenta menace." This perennial weed has vigorously naturalized itself in marshes and wet meadows throughout central North America, choking out native vegetation and encroaching on the territory of plants used as food, nest sites, and cover by a variety of birds, muskrats, turtles, and insects. Its scientific name, *Lythrum salicaria*, was derived from the Greek word "lythron," which means "the colour of darkened blood" (the colour of the plant's flowers), and from the Latin word "salix," which means "willow-like" (a purple loosestrife's leaf is long and narrow).

Gardeners really shouldn't be cultivating it. An individual purple loosestrife can grow up to six feet tall and four feet wide, and has the capacity to establish itself in dense stands of up to 80,000 stems per acre when conditions are appropriate. Each stem can produce up to 300,000 tiny seeds easily transported for miles by even the lightest of winds. That means that purple loosestrife growing in a backyard garden can potentially spread to a nearby wetland. Of equal concern is the fact that each plant can reproduce itself vegetatively from pieces of stems or roots, making it almost impossible to eradicate colonies of stray purple loosestrife simply by pulling out the parent plants.

Purple loosestrife was introduced to North America over a hundred years ago when cargo ships from Europe released ballast water from their holds before loading with cargo for a return voyage. That ballast water contained purple loosestrife seed that floated to shore and soon began growing throughout New England. The plant migrated north and west and can now be found growing in 26 States and in all Canadian provinces. Estimates indicate that loosestrife has overtaken millions of acres of North American wetlands, altering the biodiversity of those ecosystems. And unlike native plant species, purple loosestrife has no natural predators or diseases in North America to check its relentless migration across the continent. However, over the past several years, three European insect species have been released in a trial control program. Two of these insects will eat the seeds of purple loosestrife, and one will feed on the roots. Unfortunately, estimates indicate that it will take up to ten years for these insect predators to significantly reduce the purple loosestrife population.

Looking on the brighter side, the flowers of purple loosestrife are absolutely gorgeous! They're reddish-purple and attract honey bees; according to herbalists, a lotion made from these flowers has an astringent value and a healing effect. And purple loosestrife herbal tea has been used to soothe symptoms of dysentery, typhus, and typhoid fever. Even Charles Darwin thought highly of purple loosestrife, using it in his research to better understand cross-pollination in plants.

Other plants share the "loosestrife" name. Like purple loosestrife, they're vigorous growers but none are infringing on wetlands, and all are prize plants for perennial gardens.

Take the beautiful yellow loosestrife (*Lysimachia punctata*). It's in the Primrose family of plants so is not even distantly related to purple loosestrife. Named by Greek botanist and physician Dioscorides, after King Lysimachus of Thrace, yellow loosestrife has striking spires of yellow flowers that bloom in June and early July. These hardy perennials will grow well in a variety of soil conditions, in either sun or partial shade, never succumbing to disease, insect attacks, or drought.

Then there is *Lysimachia clethroides*, or gooseneck loosestrife. This plant's somewhat uncontrolled rhizome growth can cause it to quickly overrun a garden border. But when planted by itself in a sunny site, where it doesn't matter what it might crowd out, gooseneck loosestrife will reward a gardener with graceful arches of tiny white blossoms that make excellent cut flowers.

A final loosestrife of interest is *Lysimachia nummularia*, known commonly as creeping loosestrife or moneywort. It's a beautiful prostrate vine with small, one-inch, round leaves that resemble coins. Often used as an accent plant in hanging baskets and window boxes, creeping loosestrife is hardy to Zone 3, making it suitable for perennial gardens in most Maritime provinces, and it has cheery, yellow flowers that bloom all summer.

So not all "loosestrifes" are the same; the name can be deceiving. Gardeners should only be leery of the purple ones—our wetlands will be the better for it.

Creating a Butterfly Garden

Butterflies are enchanting insects. Whether flitting through the air over lawn and garden, or wafting their colourful wings while perching on the petals of a flower, no other insects appear as lovely and delicate as butterflies. To enjoy more than the rare specimen that might happen to light in the backyard or fly by on a gust of wind, gardeners can devote a section of the garden or patio plantings to attract more of these charming creatures each summer. Transforming a garden into an environment appropriate for butterflies is becoming a popular hobby among plant lovers.

There are nearly twenty thousand species of butterflies worldwide. Individuals are identified by wing colours and markings, as well as by body shapes and sizes. Butterflies go through four distinct stages in their life cycles, each accompanied by a distinct appearance that can be used for identification purposes. It all begins with eggs. For most species, these hatch within a week of being deposited by adults, though some can lie dormant through the winter months to hatch in the spring.

Eggs hatch into butterfly larvae or caterpillars, "eating machines" that munch on all parts of their host plants. Courting butterflies means that gardeners have to plant a little extra so they'll have food to support this caterpillar stage of their lifecycle.

Butterfly caterpillars have distinctive feeding patterns. They might be found on the undersides of leaves to get protection from the sun and from enemies. Or they might develop spines or hairs on their backs so that they're safer even if feeding on the tops or edges of leaves (very few predators are interested in eating a hairy or prickly lunch)!

Caterpillars molt several times before entering a chrysalis stage, which is really the cocoon in which the mature butterfly is formed. Most butterflies hatch from their chrysalises after two weeks, but some remain enclosed for the harsh winter months to hatch the following season. Butterflies that overwinter their eggs or their chrysalises do not migrate, but are able to remain in the same habitat year round. Unlike caterpillars, adult butterflies feed on nectar from flowers. At the end of their life span, they lay eggs, thus bringing the cycle full circle.

Unlike the caterpillar stage, adult butterflies feed on nectar from flowers. At the end of their life span, they lay eggs, thus bringing the life cycle full circle.

The essentials of a butterfly garden are sunlight, basking and roosting spots, shelter, puddles, and nectar and food. Butterflies are most active in sunny areas, because they need to have their wings warmed before they can fly. They enjoy basking in the sun on large, flat stones or patio blocks. Because they can't drink from open water, butterflies seek out moist areas or shallow puddles where they can sip from damp earth. Late in the day butterflies find a camouflaged roosting spot where they can spend the night, hidden from predators.

Butterflies also need protection from wind and rain. Flowering shrubs are the shelter of choice, but fences, trellises, vines, or rock walls all provide adequate protection from the elements and provide sites for egg laying or chrysalis formation.

Finally, butterflies need an assortment of plants to provide them with sources of nectar and food. Most butterfly nectar sources have fragrant, tubular flowers arranged to provide a landing and perching space. Some butterflies have short proboscises (feeding mouthparts) so prefer short-tubed flowers. Other species have long proboscises and are attracted to flowers with long tubes. Most butterflies will not climb down into a flower if it will result in damage to their wings.

Caterpillars usually seek out a limited number of food plants, eating the foliage, not the nectar. The following plants will keep both adult butterflies and larval caterpillars happy in the garden.

Plants for a New Brunswick Butterfly Garden

Food Type	Botanical Name	Common Name
NECTAR SOURCES:	*Ageratum* sp.	ageratum
	Mondarda didyma	beebalm
	Cosmos sp.	cosmos
	Echinacea purpurea	purple coneflower
	Lobelia sp.	trailing lobelia
	Lantana camara	common lantana
	Phlox	phlox
	Chrysanthemum superbum	shasta daisy
	Zinnia sp.	zinnia
	Buddleia davidii	butterfly bush
	Syringa vulgaris	lilac
	Spirea sp.	spirea
	Rhus typhina	sumac
	Weigela sp.	weigela
	Aster sp.	Michaelmas daisy
	Centaurea cyanus	cornflower
	Taraxacum officinale	dandelion
	Solidago sp.	goldenrod
	Daucus carrota	Queen Anne's lace
	Eupatorium maculatum	Joe-pye weed
	Lysimachia punctata	yellow loosestrife

Food Type	Botanical Name	Common Name
CATERPILLAR FOOD:	*Tropaeolum majus*	nasturtium
	Brassica sp.	cabbage
	Brassica oleraceae	broccoli
	Daucus carrota	carrot
	Lupinus officinale	lupine
	Plantago major	plantain
	Trifolium rubrum	red clover
	Althea sp.	hollyhock
	Prunus sp.	plum
	Prunus sp.	cherry
	Malus sylvestris	apple
	Cornus sericea	red osier dogwood
	Fraxinus americana	ash
	Populus tremuloides	poplar
	Ulmus americana	American elm
	Betula papyraceus	paper birch
	Salix sp.	willow

Perennials

Vivian Wilcox, Nashwaaksis

ANNUALS

"To be overcome by the fragrance of flowers is a delectable form of defeat."

Beverly Nichols

Annuals can quickly transform a colourless, bare spot in the garden to a vibrant landscape of orange, red, yellow, blue, or any shade in between—literally within hours if blooming, nursery-grown plants are used. Annuals selected for hanging baskets and window boxes are also instantaneous injections of colour, particularly if containers are purchased pre-planted. And, once planted, annuals are valued for their plethora of blossoms all summer long.

I use annuals in a variety of ways in my garden. I always put marigolds as companion plants between my tomato and broccoli, to help protect them from insect damage; companion planting really seems to work. (I use the small, flowered French marigold in the Boy series because they bloom prolifically and only grow to heights of 15 cm).

I also like to put Alaska Mixed nasturtiums in a sunny spot beside the basement door where there is poor, sandy soil. These nasturtiums have brightly-coloured blossoms and light green, cream-striped foliage. The old saying that "you have to be nasty to nasturtiums" is correct because the better the soil they're in, the fewer flowers they produce; they thrive in the nastiness of heat and drought.

Placing a few annuals at the base of my climbing rose bushes keeps the spot interesting after the roses finish their bloom period. I also like to put annuals in pots on the back deck, especially morning glories, which I train up a tripod of bamboo poles.

Although I never leave out old-fashioned annuals like love-lies-bleeding, petunias, cornflowers, sweet peas, poppies, heliotrope or nigella, I try new releases each summer, just to see how they'll perform; I've been impressed with osteospermum, dimorphotheca, scaveola, flowering tobacco, schizanthus, and all of the new varieties of fuchsia. I love dwarf sunflowers and climbing nasturtiums. I like to plant annual ornamental grasses (like briza, hare's tail, or sorghum) and to grow flowers for drying (statice, helichrysum, larkspur). It's also great to plant a few edible annuals (like johnny-jump-ups) for candying, adding to fruit salad, or floating in punch.

Annual flowering plants are appealing for a variety of reasons. The gardeners in this chapter have their own reasons for making room for these plants in their gardens.

VIVIAN WILCOX
NASHWAAKSIS

Vivian Wilcox likes to experiment in her garden and that's one of the biggest reasons for her love of annuals. They allow her to mix and match colour schemes and flower types each year, so she can keep flexibility in her planting scheme. Because one seed packet can produce hundreds of plants, she finds annuals economical to grow. They also make great bouquets—both fresh and dried—and they bloom repeatedly all summer long. Finally, Vivian finds she has more choice of plant material to work with when she selects annuals because she can order from any number of seed catalogues, rather than being restricted to picking up common varieties at a local nursery.

When Vivian started her garden over a decade ago, on a city lot in the Nashwaaksis area of Fredericton, she was dealing with a bare landscape and the poor, substandard topsoil typical of housing developments. She couldn't get grass to grow well because there was so little organic matter and nutrients in the ground to help establish a healthy root system. She had drainage problems in places because the soil was so compacted that water couldn't percolate through it. And she was a novice gardener who wasn't sure what fertilizers to use or what plants to put where.

Through trial and error, the help of a few good books on gardening, and with advice from fellow enthusiasts in the Fredericton Garden Club, Vivian slowly transformed her landscape into a healthy environment for vigorous plant growth. She started by making a compost pile and adding this material to her garden soil. Initially she took great pains to get the compost mixed thoroughly into the garden, but in recent years she has only sprinkled it on the surface. "If you think about the forest floor," says Vivian, "where composting is taking place naturally all of the time, you realize that Mother Nature doesn't turn compost into the soil." So she takes the same approach and simply lets the rain take the compost nutrients down into the soil for her.

As another part of her initial landscape preparation, Vivian made regular assessments of her soil's pH level. pH is a measure of acidity and alkalinity, measured on a scale from 1 to 14; numbers below 7 refer to an acid or sour soil, while numbers above 7 refer to an alkaline or sweet soil. A pH of 7 is completely neutral. pH levels affects the availability of nutrients in soil and therefore play a role in overall plant health. The best pH level for growing lawn grass is around 6.5; most annuals and perennials prefer a soil pH between 6 and 6.5. Gardeners can have their soil pH levels checked at government soils labs or by purchasing a pH kit at a garden centre.

Because Vivian's soil has always been somewhat acidic, she makes annual applications of lime over her lawn and in many of her flower beds. However, her woodlands garden at the back of the house has ferns, rhododendrons, and azalea, and these are plants that prefer an acidic soil, so she avoids treating these with lime.

This work to improve her soil's organic-matter content and pH level means she now has great success with just about anything she chooses to grow. Her garden includes many types of trees and shrubs, and dozens of species of perennials; it's annuals she loves, though, and she plants great numbers of them each spring. "They give an ongoing colour," she says, "especially when my perennials have completed their bloom time." And the combination of annuals and perennials gives her landscape an authentic "cottage garden" look.

Most of Vivian's annuals are sown directly in the garden. This way, she avoids the work involved in transplanting seedlings. And seeding directly in the garden is perfect for annuals like sweet alyssum, ageratum, marigolds, calendula, and clarkia—all species that reach blooming size in a matter of weeks. "Some gardeners find that it takes too long for annuals to produce blooms if they're directly seeded in the garden," says Vivian, "but the trick is to wait until the soil is really warm before sowing." In warm soil, the seeds germinate quickly and, because they don't have the setback of being transplanted, they tend to 'catch up' to annuals that have been started earlier indoors and set out at the start of the gardening season. The only exceptions to this wait-for-warm-soil rule are sweet peas and shirley poppies (Vivian's favourite annuals). Sweet peas thrive in cool conditions, so seeds can be sown as soon as the ground can be worked each spring. "I love to pick bouquets of sweet peas to give to those who visit my garden," she explains, "and I enjoy their fragrance wafting through the air!" Vivian grows the old-fashioned varieties that reach heights of two metres, and trains them to a trellis against the sides of her potting shed. There are also bush varieties of sweet peas, which grow to heights of 40 centimetres or less, needing no support at all. When flowers are routinely cut from the plant, sweet peas will continue to bloom for most of the summer.

Vivian's much-loved shirley poppies produce ornate seed capsules when they finish blooming and, after they dry naturally on the plant, she collects these capsules to save for the next season. But she doesn't wait until spring to sow these seeds; instead, she sprinkles them on the soil in late fall each year, so they get an early start at germinating in the spring. The seeds tolerate New Brunswick winters very well, and this autumn-sowing method means an early appearance of poppies in the garden each summer.

Some annuals do get a head start indoors because they take a long time to reach the blooming stage. Vivian sows these plants (like impatiens, geraniums, petunias, larkspur, and asters) in recycled margarine or yogurt containers with holes poked in the bottom to ensure good drainage. She also uses home-made pots made from newspaper; these are easy and inexpensive to construct. Vivian begins by tearing newspaper into wide strips, which she wraps around the end of a broom handle several times. When the layers are pulled off the handle, one end is pressed flat to create a small tubular "pot." Next, in an old glass casserole dish or roasting pan, she places enough of these to hold each other up, and then she fills them with sterile potting mix. Seedlings grown in these newspaper sleeves can be put directly into the garden, paper and all, because the "pot" will quickly degrade.

Over the years, Vivian has regularly changed the look of her garden by moving her planting sites. She has found a great way to put in new beds, with minimum effort. "When I'm making a new area for planting," she says, "I don't dig out the grass." Instead, she places a garden hose down on the lawn and moves it around until she gets the shape and size she's looking for. Then she digs a trench, following the outline of the hose, in which she inserts rubber edging. After that, she puts a 15 cm layer of leaves, grass clippings, or other garden waste over the entire area, covering this with thick sections of moist newspaper. Finally, she adds a top layer of chopped leaves mixed with compost. This is left to decompose over the next few months, resulting in a ready-to-plant garden with no sod removal required. "There's no tilling necessary," says Vivian, "and you don't need a strong back or arms to get the bed prepared." After plants are put in place the next year, Vivian adds lots of mulch to keep weeds under control. She doesn't like landscape fabric, especially for the areas where she grows annuals, because it makes it difficult to work in the soil underneath. She also finds that the fabric doesn't let rain penetrate down into the plants' roots as well as a layer of mulch.

Because she makes a point of frequent deadheading, Vivian's annuals add brightness to her garden all summer long. In late August, though, she lets many varieties mature to produce seeds, which she'll gather for the next season. "This doesn't work for hybrids," she warns. Hybrid varieties of annuals usually aren't able to produce seeds at all; if they do manage to produce a few, the seeds are usually sterile. Even if a hybrid does produce fertile seed, this never grows into a plant that looks exactly like the parent. That means that a gardener who grows hybrids needs to buy fresh seed each year.

These gathered seeds are stored in labelled envelopes in the refrigerator. There they stay until the following spring, providing her with an economical source of material for the next planting season. "I sometimes don't use them all," she says, "because I might substitute a new type of annual that I've seen in a catalogue and am anxious to try." But that's the beauty of annuals: "I can pick different colours or varieties each year, and I can change where they're planted, and how many of each I want to grow."

Stephen Stephenson
Jacksonville

It would appear that Stephen Stephenson has more people to help him enjoy his garden than do most gardeners. His property runs along the Trans-Canada highway in Jacksonville, New Brunswick, which leaves it pretty much open to public inspection. When daffodils and tulips are in bloom in the spring, passersby stop to help Stephen admire them. And when the lupins are at their peak, another set of visitors comes along to

Stephen Stephenson's woodwork (such as this well-dressed unicyclist) decorates his Jacksonville garden.

stroll over the lawn and remind him that his gardens are absolutely delightful. Of course the lupins are followed by the lilies, and the lilies followed by a huge display of annuals. In fact, the garden is really never without a wealth of blossoms and a tourist or two stopping in for a peek and a picture.

It's hard to believe that Stephen hasn't been a gardener for all of his eighty-three years. But it wasn't until after his retirement in 1984 that he decided gardening would be a good way for him to keep physically fit. Since then, he's had plenty of exercise maintaining his two-acre property. From early in the spring until late in the fall, his spare time is spent sowing seeds, pulling weeds, staking, pruning, watering and hoeing in his flower beds and his large vegetable garden. Not only does he enjoy the colour of all those flowers, but he grows all of the fresh tomatoes, potatoes, beans, squash, and cucumbers that he and his wife can eat. Some seeds that he plants are ones he has gathered and saved year after year. One tall bean pole, supported by guy wires at the side of the vegetable garden, is covered with pods of a unique colour. "They've been in the family for years," he says, when asked about their speckled, creamy yellow colour. "You can't beat the flavour, even when they're past their prime!" he offers with pride. "I'll save you some seed."

Each year, Stephen plants scarlet runner beans along the front of the house, and trains them up strings suspended from the roof. Although many people consider scarlet runners great for eating, Stephen prefers them for their bright red flowers. On their best days," he says, "the vines grow four inches in just one hour. You can almost see them moving!"

Planting a large collection of annual flowers is another form of exercise for Stephen. Many of these are grown in large, rectangular beds—full of lavatera, cosmos, calendula, and sunflowers—laid out in sequence between the house and the highway. The cosmos are up to 110 cm in height, with single flowers, feathery foliage. Their pink, white, and rose-coloured blossoms blend in nicely with clusters of white and burgundy hollyhocks, and with perennials such as gaillardia, purple coneflower, phlox, and matricaria. If cosmos blossoms are regularly deadheaded, plants will keep blooming until autumn frost; if left to mature, they'll have interesting seed heads (which Stephen collects to sow again the next season). Cosmos also come in dwarf varieties, which only reach heights of 25 cm; or varieties like Sea Shells cosmos, which have unusual tubular petals. Any type of cosmos makes a great cutflower, and they complement Stephen's profuse, deep pink lavatera. As lavatera hate to be transplanted, he sows them directly in the garden after the soil warms in the spring. Gardeners who prefer to start their lavatera indoors—for earlier blossoms—should sow each seed in its own container, rather than in a flat (where roots can tangle and break when single plants are pulled apart). Peat pots are great, as are the plug trays that you get bedding plants in from a nursery.

The calendula in Stephen's garden come up on their own each year, wherever they please. Although considered annuals, their seeds overwinter with great success in New Brunswick gardens, and often it's necessary to weed them out to make room for something else. (It's not nice to call them weeds, but the definition of a weed is anything that grows where it isn't wanted.)

Finally, sunflowers in the Stephenson garden give birds and squirrels something to nibble on. Like the calendula, most tall sunflowers re-seed themselves on a regular basis each year. But Stephen does plant seeds of some dwarf types (like Teddy Bear) that only grow to heights of 45 cm.

What Stephen likes best about all of these annuals is that they reach their peak bloom time just when the surrounding perennials are past their prime. It's always perfect timing, and it makes the Stephenson garden a non-stop riot of flowers, and a drawing card for the travelling public. Even if people drive past—because they haven't been able to get stopped in time to properly pull into the driveway—they usually turn around and come back, just to take a closer look. Stephen wonders what all the fuss is about, because when he looks at the marvellous display, he always sees something that needs deadheading, dividing, or digging out. He smiles when offered a compliment, but says that "there's really too much for one person to do, although not enough for two, so everything only gets about half done."

Visitors to the garden also enjoy Stephen's woodworking talents, seen in the lifelike wooden figures that decorate the property. At the end of the driveway, for example, is a well-dressed man riding a unicycle and waving a Canadian flag, accompanied by a spotted dog; a motor attached to the bottom of the unicycle's wheel makes it appear as if the cyclist is actually riding away after a spin round the garden. Other wooden models include a contented cow being milked by a mild-mannered maid, a young boy sitting on a barrel with his fishing pole, and another jauntily-clad man with a golf club, about make the next hole in one. Bird boxes and painted rocks complete a garden that brings Stephen Stephenson year-round work and pleasure, and gives travellers a rare horticultural treat.

Beverly Corey
Welshpool

As a child, Beverly Corey summered on Campobello Island. It was a time for carefree, sunny days by the sea, just like holidays should be. Little did she know that—many years later—she'd return to live permanently in the lovely cottage that had once been her family's summer retreat. The homey white building sits on a piece of land between the island's North Road and the Bay of Fundy shoreline, and is thought to have been constructed by a sea captain over a century ago. Surrounded by trees and hedgerows, it has an expanse of lawn at the back, where Beverly and her husband Ivan sit and watch the setting sun, just as she did in her youth on warm summer evenings.

The Corey cottage is screened from the road by a white picket fence, three metres high. Not only does this structure give their home some privacy, but it also serves as a lovely backdrop for hardy red rugosa roses that bloom all summer long. Beverly loves roses and has transplanted many from the island's beaches and roadsides, where they grow wild in great abundance.

Hugging the cottage's foundation, and scattered here and there in the backyard, are beds of cultivated and native plant species. There's a huge horse chestnut tree, an old-fashioned lilac grown to tree-like proportions, and a gigantic spruce that shades a good portion of the lawn. "That spruce used to be my height," remembers Beverly, as she looks up at the giant it has become.

Throughout the garden are beach stones, along with collectibles like bird feeders, lanterns, and ornate crockery pots. A birdbath provides water for feathered visitors, a Victorian gazing ball awaits the admiring faces of garden guests, and unusual pieces of driftwood poke their way through the greenery. Granite blocks have been used as edging, and weathered bricks from the cottage's original chimney are stacked to anchor the sides of a planting bed.

One of the most interesting annual wildflowers that grows abundantly both in Beverly's garden and all over adjacent properties and roadsides is the Himalayan balsam. Native to Europe, this plant can be found in many seaside locations throughout southern New Brunswick. It first began growing here centuries ago, when seeds were released in the ballast water of cargo ships that called at ports along North America's eastern seaboard. Himalayan balsam grows to heights of a metre or more, pro-

Beverly and Ivan Corey start some annuals in their homemade "standing greenhouse," which protects seedlings from island breezes.

ducing attractive clusters of purple-pink blooms during mid to late July. It's a relative of the spotted touch-me-not, a wildflower that grows in marshes and wet areas in the province. Both plants have long, fat seed pods that tend to "pop" when mature, spreading seeds long distances. Luckily, Himalayan balsam can easily be kept under control by mowing or by pulling seedlings out by the roots as they appear each spring.

A colourful collection of annual bedding plants accompany all of the native species in Beverly's garden. These annuals can be found in beds, planters, and hanging baskets all around the property, especially at the doorway to the cottage, where they make a welcoming sight for visitors. Growing in beds near the front of the house are nasturtiums, purple wave petunias, and lemon gem marigolds. Each of these species form mounds of colour that last throughout the summer; they're outlined by more bricks from the cottage's old chimney. Hanging from the eves of the canopy over the front entrance is a basket full of soft pink impatiens; the basket shares this elevated spot with a lobster trap buoy, a collection of bells on a piece of fishing rope, and a wind chime made from old spoons. A pot of pink and mauve petunias sits on a wicker table on the porch steps, and a planter full of maroon pansies rests atop a jet-black stool. Attached to the wall of the cottage is a wicker basket full of purple petunias and german ivy, while an urn of white-flowered calla lilies rests on the ground in front of a porch pillar. (Beverly overwinters these lilies each year on an indoor window ledge, and is always pleased to see them flower each summer, after she moves them outdoors.) Glass fishing net floats of various sizes and colours sit on the deck of the porch, adding additional nautical flair to the potted plants. And a glider chair stands ready for anyone wanting to rest and enjoy more time looking over Beverly's garden.

Most of these annuals were transplants from nurseries that Beverly loves to visit at the beginning of the garden season. However, some annuals were started in her new "standing greenhouse," which Ivan fashioned after one they'd seen in a garden centre. It consists of a platform (approximately two-and-a-half metres long by one metre wide) with a number of arched hoops over top. The hoops support a covering of clear plastic, which can be opened to allow Beverly to water and monitor the plants underneath, or closed to create a mini-solarium for growing seedlings. It's just the right size for her to start some of her annuals and vegetable garden transplants, especially basil, her favourite herb. And the standing greenhouse is also perfect for protecting seedlings from heavy breezes. "An island gardener always has wind to contend with," says Beverly. Then again, putting up with a bit of wind would be worth it—just to be able to garden in such a delightful spot!

Mary White
Garden Gate Nursery
Carlow

A bouquet of flowers has always been a symbol of joy, love, and living beauty. And although a florist is usually where one goes to make their selections these days, a bouquet fresh from the summer garden is even more appealing. That's why Mary White decided to open a cutflower farm. She loved going to her flowerbeds for blossoms, and these bouquets were always bringing compliments from those who envied her luck at having access to such delightful blooms. So Mary decided that it made sense to share her good fortune by opening her gardens to those interested in picking their own bouquet from the wide selection of flowers planted around her home. She also started to create floral arrangements for weddings and parties. As one thing led to another, Mary found herself erecting two large greenhouses; this way, she could not only get a head start on plants for her cutflower gardens, but also offer customers annual bedding plants, perennials, vegetable transplants, and herbs. That's how "Garden Gate Nursery" was begun in Carlow, New Brunswick.

Mary didn't grow up as a gardener. Her childhood was spent on a large farm in New Brunswick's potato belt, where so much time was involved in planting and tending farm crops that "we were lucky to get red dahlias across the front of the house." Now that she has started her own nursery and cutflower farm, she feels that not being exposed to gardening while she was young has been both a blessing and a curse. She readily admits that her lack of gardening experience resulted in her venturing ahead with things that she might not have done if she'd known better in the first place. And it has meant that she has faced some disappointments and lost time and expense. But she has also had some great learning experiences on the road to making Garden Gate Nursery a success. "My planting is often trial and error," she confesses, "but I always learn something from the work."

Mary started her first gardens in 1983, when she and her husband built a home on what was part of her grandparents' farm. It was essentially in the middle of a hayfield, several kilometres northwest of Bristol, with no trees for shade and with very shallow, rocky soil. But she was anxious to grow some flowers and decided that the best approach was to build a series of raised beds. She constructed them in various lengths, but each was kept to just over three metres wide, so that she could easily reach their

At Mary White's Garden Gate Nursery, you can pick flowers to create your own bouquet.

centres from either side, which made planting and weeding manageable. She filled the beds with a mixture of topsoil and compost, to a depth of approximately 25 cm. And she started a row of pine trees behind the beds to act as a windbreak and to trap snow during the winter (for added protection from exposure).

Most of Mary's beds were devoted to annuals because she finds them to be perfect for bouquets. She cultivates many of the most popular types of annuals, including marigolds, petunias, and geraniums, but she also grows some of the less common varieties, such as larkspur, nigella, baby's breath, statice, blue salvia, celosia, and love-lies-bleeding. All of these produce excellent flowers for air drying. Mary has done more drying in the last few summers in order to have material for creating everlasting bouquets and dried flower arrangements for her decorating contracts. After the greenhouse has been emptied in late June, she converts it into a large drying room by lining the inside with large sheets of black fabric to keep out the light, and by setting up fans to move in fresh air. She has found that this makes an excellent location for transforming fresh flowers into everlastings. "It's important to have warmth, darkness, and good air circulation, so that flowers dry quickly but retain their "just-picked colour!" But it's equally important to know when to pick flowers with respect to the stage of flower development and the time of day. "I have found that the best time to pick most flowers is just as they are beginning to open," she describes, " and I try to do it mid-morning, after the dew has dried off the petals and foliage." Globe thistle is one of her favourite perennial flowers for drying, and she watches it closely when buds start to appear because the flowers will tend to shatter while drying if picked at too late a growth stage. Peonies are picked when their flowers are just cupped, and liatris are cut before all of the blossoms on the stalk are fully open.

Mary suspends individual stems of large blooms like sunflowers by attaching their stalks with clothespins to wires that run along the length of the greenhouse. She gathers other flowers in small bouquets and holds them together with elastic bands. She finds this better than using string or twist ties because stems tend to shrink as they dry, and the elastic shrinks with them, keeping individual stems from slipping out of the cluster. These bouquets are suspended from wires in the greenhouse and from chickenwire mesh stretched along the benches.

As time progressed, Mary started planting perennials, like daylilies, purple coneflowers, lilies, peonies, delphiniums, heuchera, iris, phlox, tulips, and daffodils in a bed that runs along the driveway at the front of the house. This offers her clients another collection of blooms to incorporate into bouquets of annuals.

For the last five years, Mary has built up a devoted clientele for both her cutflowers and her plant sales. Each spring, she starts hundreds of flats of annuals in time for them to be in a blooming stage when customers come to her nursery. "I find that the material has to be in flower in order for people to be comfortable with what they're buying," she says, and she sets her planting schedule accordingly. Species that require longer periods of time to bloom are started in her germination room, in the basement of her home. (She has a series of grow lights and shelves there, and provides extra moisture in the air with the help of a small, portable humidifier.) Species that need less time to grow to a flowering stage are started directly in the greenhouse in late March.

In addition to preparing flats of annuals for sale at her nursery, Mary often grows a few varieties like cosmos, sunflowers, and impatiens in individual pots. That way they can get a bit larger and are more perfectly formed. She charges more for these special potted plants, but customers appreciate their more mature look, particularly if they are to be used for patio planters or window boxes.

After spring sales start to wind down, Mary devotes her time to setting annuals out in the garden. Her cutflowers customers have already been calling, keen to collect bouquets of daffodils and tulips. From then until fall, flower enthusiasts arrive to have Mary help them collect bouquets for church services and community events. Knowing that her flowers are being enjoyed by so many people makes Mary's work that much more rewarding; she's been able to spread her love of colour and bloom far beyond the borders of her garden.

The Secrets of Gardening with Annuals

- Plant annuals if you want a different look to your garden each year.
- Check your soil pH, and add lime if it's too acidic.
- Sow varieties of annuals that take a long time to the reach blooming stage indoors, so that they'll have a head start at the beginning of the gardening season.
- Sow quick-to-bloom annuals directly in the garden, but wait until the soil warms up.
- Plant sunflowers to attract birds to your garden.
- Cover the sides of tool sheds or garages with annual vines like climbing nasturtiums, scarlet runner beans, sweet peas, morning glories, or cobaea.
- Use mulch rather than landscape fabric to keep weeds under control in annual beds.
- Keep annuals deadheaded to encourage repeat blooming.

Good Garden Flowers for Drying

Botanical Name	Common Name
Artemesia sp.	artemesia
Solidago sp.	goldenrod
Clematis ap.	clematis
Viola tricolor	pansy
Achillea sp.	yarrow
Allium sp.	lady's mantle
Delphinium sp.	delphinium
Gypsophila sp.	baby's breath
Helichrysum sp.	strawflower
Consolida ambigua	larkspur
Lavendula sp.	lavender
Nigella	nigella
Amaranthus sp.	love-lies-bleeding
Celosia sp.	cockscomb flower
Paeonia sp.	peony
Rosa sp.	rose
Tagetes sp.	marigold
Papaver sp.	poppy (seed heads)

Edible Annuals

A large number of the annual flower species that are favourites with New Brunswick gardeners are *edible* and can add flavour, texture, colour, and general interest to soups, salads, cakes, cookies, and more. By making flowers a part of a meal, you can have your bouquet and eat it, too! The only things to be cautious of when using flowers as food is to be sure of their proper identity and make sure they haven't been sprayed with a pesticide. Here are some suggestions for making annuals a part of your diet:

- Whole blossoms of annual carnations can be used to garnish desserts or fruit punches.
- Pansies are great for pressing into the frosting on top of a child's birthday cake.
- Hybrid Tea rose petals are lovely in fruit salad, especially if they are collected early in the day, when they have the most fragrance and intense colour.
- Nasturtium flowers, with a peppery taste much like watercress, can add flavour to herb butters, cheese spreads, dips, sandwiches, omelets, sauces, salads, and rice dishes.
- Borage blossoms have shades of pink and blue, making them attractive to freeze in ice cubes or rings for keeping a summer drink cool.
- Fuchsia flower petals are terrific for incorporating into the batter of a cake, or for adding to fruit salad.
- Snapdragon blossoms make colourful additions to a salad of tossed greens.
- Bright red geranium flowers, when separated into their individual florets, can be added to the custard in summer trifles.
- Marigold petals are real taste-bud teasers when mixed with mesculin greens and dressed with a simple vinaigrette.

Candied Flowers

Bring one cup of white sugar and 1/4 cup of water to a boil for two minutes. Add 1/4 teaspoon almond extract. Let the mixture cool. Add freshly-picked (but dry) blossoms of edible flowers, a few at a time, and let them stay in the syrup for one minute. Make sure that each flower is completely coated with syrup. Remove flowers to wax paper and let them dry thoroughly. Store the results in a glass jar.

Ken Peck, Island View

FRUIT

"What can your eye desire to see, your ears to hear, your mouth to taste or your nose to smell, that is not to be had in an orchard?"

William Lawson, 1618

My grandfather James H. Dunphy was a dairy farmer and a Saint John River Valley fruit grower with a large commercial apple orchard planted in familiar varieties like McIntosh, Cortland, Melba, New Brunswicker, Alexander and Dudley Winter. When he wasn't milking cows or haying, he would be tending the orchard. In late winter, he would spent weeks doing the pruning that helps keep apple trees to bear well. All summer he'd mow the grass between the rows of trees, spraying against insects and disease, and readying picking bins and ladders for the harvest. From late August until well into November he would spend every day, all day, in the trees, picking the fruits of his labours. And what hard work it was!

In addition to apple, there were also a few pear and sour cherry trees in my grandfather's orchard. It always amazed me to be able to pick a pear right off a tree, because there weren't that many hardy varieties in New Brunswick, back in those days. And being able to pop bright red cherries in my mouth, even though they were very sour, was an equally novel treat.

My grandfather tended a raspberry patch, some gooseberry bushes, and a few high-bush cranberries as well. I spent many summers helping him harvest these fruits and watching my grandmother turn them into jams, jellies, preserves, and delicious desserts.

My family and I now live and garden on what was part of my grandparent's farm. Perhaps that's why I've always tried to produce various types of fruit, just to keep up with tradition. I've branched out a bit, so to speak, and not only have apple and pear trees, along with raspberries and high-bush cranberries, but I also grow lingon berries, grapes, kiwis, blueberries, strawberries, blackberries, and both red and black currants. However, I haven't been able to bring myself to plant gooseberries. All those childhood sessions of "tipping and tailing" in my grandmother's kitchen (taking off the inedible top and bottom of each gooseberry) made me vow never to have anything to do with this plant again.

But I'm not the only one growing fruit in the home garden; it's becoming a popular practice across New Brunswick. The following gardeners, including my husband Ken (our family's raspberry expert) are good examples of modern-day fruit growers.

MARGIE ANN AND DALBERT BOYD DOUGLAS

Back in the nineteenth century, plant hunters were dispatched, by the European aristocracy, all around the world to seek out both wild and cultivated plants that might be profitable and productive. Somewhere in Korea, Manchuria, or perhaps Japan, they came upon a smooth-skinned, sweet, green fruit, about the size of a large grape, growing from sturdy vines. Fortunately, they collected these plants, which eventually made their way to the nurseries of North America. Today, these super-hardy kiwi—first cousins of the famous, hairy kiwi (*Actinidia deliciosa*) that we have all seen in grocery stores—are available for planting in Canadian gardens. They're disease and pest free,

Margie Ann Boyd has been growing hardy kiwis in her backyard for years.

have handsome foliage on vigorous vines, and are prolific producers after only a few short years in the garden. Best of all, the clusters of fruit can be eaten whole, like grapes, without being peeled, and even New Zealanders have admitted to their distinctly kiwi flavour!

Margie Ann and Dalbert Boyd have been growing hardy kiwis in their backyard for many years. Their property is on a south-facing slope, overlooking the Saint John River in Douglas, just west of Fredericton. Their garden is home to many common types of fruit-producing plants like apple trees, raspberry canes, currants, strawberries, and rhubarb, all of which are grown using organic methods. Being adventurous gardeners, the Boyds decided to try growing kiwis when they first became available at Canadian nurseries almost a decade ago.

"They were just little, bitty things when we first bought them," says Dalbert, "so we thought that we'd need at least four plants to cover the arbour that we were going to plant them beside." They chose two males and two females, because hardy kiwi are "dioecious"—there are separate male and female plants. In some cases, especially if the plants are growing in calcareous soils, it's possible to recognize the male kiwis because they are beautifully variegated with blotches of white and pink. However, these attractive leaves are only found on one of the two species of kiwi that are hardy in cold climates—the *Actinidia kolomikta*, or Arctic kiwi, which is extremely cold tolerant and able to survive winter temperature as low as -40° C. This species will grow best in full sun, where its roots are shaded from the strong afternoon rays. Arctic kiwi vines grow to lengths of ten metres.

The second type of hardy kiwi is *Actinidia arguta*, commonly known as "bower vine." This species is slightly less hardy than its Arctic cousin, but will still survive temperatures of -30° C. Vines can be up to 18 metres in length if the plant is placed in a sunny location, but leaves are not variegated. Without leaf markings it's usually difficult to tell a male kiwi plant from a female one, unless you know what anatomical structures to look for in the flower when each gender is blooming. Fortunately, nurseries will have their plants clearly marked. It's generally recommended that gardeners purchase one male to provide sufficient pollen for up to nine females.

Once the kiwis started to grow, the Boyds quickly realized that they had sufficient plants to cover the arbour. Vines grew rapidly after the plants became established and because kiwi vines are twisters, they twined themselves nicely around the framework of the arbour, completely obliterating the structure from view. "I worked composted chicken manure into the soil around their roots for the first few years," explains Dalbert, "but after that, the plants seemed to grow vigorously without it." He continues to water them with compost tea, just as they start to flower each spring, but other than that he leaves the plants to fend for themselves.

"They're very easy to look after," he admits. He finds the plants to be disease and insect resistant and so hardy that they don't need any winter protection. "I don't put evergreen boughs over their roots or anything over their branches," he says, "but we do have them growing in a relatively protected spot." Gardeners who plant kiwi in more exposed locations might consider covering the base of the vines with boughs, just in case the winter brings little snow. And in the event of the forecast of late spring frosts, it's a good idea to cover vines overnight with a tarp or cloth sheet; kiwi leaf out and produce flower buds early in the growing season, so they need some cover when the weather forecast calls for frosty temperatures.

Margie Ann does remember a funny story about their early years of growing kiwi. "We noticed pale pink blotches on some of the leaves," she recalls, "and took great pains to remove them whenever they appeared, thinking they were the result of some sort of disease!" But now the couple know those "blotches" are the natural leaf variegation of the male kiwi plant, and recall their leaf-picking activity with smiles.

The only problem that Margie Ann and Dalbert have with their kiwis has nothing to do with the plants themselves. "We have lots of squirrels and birds in the garden," confesses Dalbert, "so they usually take their fair share of our harvest." That isn't too much of a hardship because the Boyd kiwis are prolific. "There's enough for the wildlife too."

Gardeners who want to plant a large number of kiwis should space the plants approximately four or five metres apart and train them to sturdy posts, arbours, or trellises. Newly-planted specimens should be kept well watered until roots become anchored in the soil. Annual applications of compost or well-rotted manure around the base of the plant are appropriate, but excess amounts will result in too much foliage and too few kiwifruit. Pruning of vegetative shoots (these are long and have nodes spaced farther apart than the shorter, fruiting vines) on mature plants can be done in late winter, to encourage flower production. You can eventually expect to harvest up to 11 kg of lush, ripe kiwifruit—per vine—in late August every year.

Bob Osborne
Corn Hill

Visions of vineyards bring to mind the verdant valleys of Italy and Germany, the famous wine regions of California, or even Canada's own fruit belts in the Niagara region of southern Ontario and the Okanagan Valley in British Columbia. These locations all have long growing seasons and mild climates that produce crops of wine, raisin, and table grapes. The grape varieties used in these places have long histories and require special cultivation, and are mostly derived from famous European grapes, with the associated tenderness and requirements for winter protection.

Thankfully, recent years have brought the release of several new, early-bearing and cold-tolerant grape cultivars, which allow more Canadian gardeners to grow this age-old fruit. Home gardeners in New Brunswick, for example, can now grow grapes for home wine making, for eating, or for producing jams and jellies. They can also grow grapes to make attractive additions to a landscape, when they are used to create a living screen over a patio or deck, along a property line or on an arbour over a garden path.

Bob Osborne is New Brunswick's best source for hardy grapes. For many years he has searched in countries throughout the northern hemisphere for obscure, short-season grape varieties. His efforts have reaped a surprisingly large number of grapes that grow well in Eastern Canada. He has tested and propagated all of them at his nursery in Corn Hill, near Sussex, and can now recommend them without reservation.

"All of the grape varieties listed in our catalogue will grow

Bob Osborne is New Brunswick's best source for hardy grapes.

well in New Brunswick," he says, "but choosing one really depends on what you're going to use the fruit for." He notes that Minnesota 78 produces a sweet grape with a flavour that reminds him of grape-flavoured bubble gum. Its fruit is great for fresh eating or for use in desserts.

Valiant is the best variety of grape for making juice. "If they're really and truly ripened—and that means leaving them on the vine until well after they have turned a deep blue colour—you can't beat Valiant grapes for juice production," he declares. Their juice can be consumed fresh or made into wine. As for the Beta cultivar, "it's like a Concord grape, but a little more tart and zippy," says Bob, who recommends this grape for making jelly.

To grow grapes well, gardeners need to pay attention to a number of things. First, they must choose an acceptable planting site. It should be a location that gets full sun, is protected from heavy winds, and has well-drained, organic-matter-rich soil with a pH of around 6.5. Second, gardeners must plant the grape vines properly. The best time to do this is in the spring but fall planting is also acceptable, especially if containerized plants are used. The vine's root ball should be placed in a planting hole that has been dug deep enough and wide enough to accommodate it, and that has had compost and bone meal added to it. "Plant the stem deeper than it was in the pot," recommends Bob, because roots will be generated on the section that is below the soil. Good topsoil should then be placed around the roots and firmly tamped in place to eliminate air pockets, and to ensure proper root-soil contact. Watering just after the vine is planted will help to settle the soil around the root ball.

A third thing that gardeners need to pay attention to in order to have success with grapes concerns pruning. A grape's first pruning can be done at planting time, when all but the most vigorous cane should be removed from the plant. This remaining cane should be cut back so that only two buds remain, thereby encouraging good root growth and limiting amounts of top growth to reduce water stress in the plant.

In subsequent years, pruning can be carried out late in the fall, after leaf drop, or very early in the spring while the plant is still dormant. The most popular pruning method is called the "four-arm kniffin system." It trains a grape to a support structure consisting of two stout posts with wires strung between them at two different levels: the first wire is approximately one metre from the ground, and the second wire is approximately 75 cm above the first. Immediately after it is planted, the central cane of the grape plant should be tied up to the top wire. If it doesn't reach this in the first season, a piece of binder twine or a bamboo cane can be used to bridge the distance. All other side growth should be snipped off. In the second and third season, four of the strongest side branches should be selected for the "arms" at locations along the stem that will allow them to be trained to grow outwards on the top and bottom wires. These side branches should be pruned so that there are only ten buds remaining along their lengths. Each year thereafter, previous fruit-bearing canes should be cut away to make room for renewed growth.

A final consideration for good grape growing relates to plant nutrition. Grapes are not heavy feeders. Too much fertilizer will actually encourage excess foliage at the expense of fruit production. So a top dressing of compost, in the spring each year, is all that's necessary to provide an adequate source of slow-release nutrients for optimum harvests.

Getting a good grape harvest is something that Bob Osborne has done often. Corn Hill Nursery has a sizeable vineyard, and each fall he invites New Brunswickers to a "Grape Fest" weekend. "It's one of our most popular events," he confesses. Those who attend get to taste freshly-picked grapes and to sample grape jams and jellies made in the Nursery's café. Seminars focusing on how grapes are grown and pruned are also offered. There's a little music and a lot of laughter. Grapes seem to bring out the best in people, especially if they're home grown.

Ken Peck
Island View

It's hard to get tired of eating fresh raspberries—they're perfect right from the bush, and sensational when served with a simple drizzle of sweet cream. They're also terrific in trifle, marvellous in muffins, pleasing in a pie, and just right when made into jam. That's why the annual raspberry harvest in Ken Peck's garden is always anticipated with great delight.

Ken planted two dozen canes of the Boyne variety of raspberries over twenty years ago at his Island View property, just west of Fredericton. "I'd never planted raspberries before," he admits "and their bare roots looked pretty dried-up to me." But he was working with dormant plants that had just come out of cold storage at the New Brunswick Department of Agriculture's facilities at Hoyt. Canes are dug in the fall and stored bare root in bins of sawdust through the winter months at this government-owned horticulture centre, so that they'll be ready for commercial growers and home gardeners to plant first thing in the spring. The plants are certified to be disease-free. "It wasn't long before the canes began leafing out," Ken recalls, and since then he's had abundant crops every year.

Raspberries grow on stiff, upright canes that are best planted in the spring in a well-drained site that will receive full sun and some protection from strong winds. The ideal time to prepare their growing area is in the fall, so that canes can be put in place as soon as the ground can be worked the next season.

The best soil for raspberry plants is that which is rich in organic matter with lots of moisture-holding capacity. These conditions can be created by working generous amounts of composted manure into a garden trench about 45 cm wide and 25 cm deep.

At planting time, raspberry canes should be buried in the trench so that their root-stem interface is approximately 10 cm below the soil surface, leaving 60 cm between plants in the row. The canes should then be cut back to 30 cm above the soil level to encourage new growth. After planting and pruning, the plants should be watered thoroughly. Raspberries require lots of moisture, especially during their first year in the garden. But they won't require additional fertilizer during their first growing season. In subsequent years they'll thrive with an early spring application of composted manure or of a balanced granular fertilizer at the rate of 3 kg per 3 linear metres of row. "I use nothing but composted chicken manure and have had great results," says Ken. "It adds organic matter as well as slow-release nutrients."

Raspberries also need to be pruned annually. Their root systems are perennial, but each year they send up new shoots which are biennial and which will not produce a crop until the second growing season. After their fruit-bearing year, raspberry canes die and need to be removed. "The easiest way for a home gardener to keep track of exactly which canes need to be cut out and which should be left in place," describes Ken, "is to prune their raspberry plants in the spring when it's easiest to tell the difference between canes that are dead and the canes that will bear fruit." Old canes are brittle and dull looking and have no new buds swelling along their length. Fruit-bearing canes are shiny, brownish green, and their stems are covered with new buds.

Ken constructed a home-made raspberry pruner by attaching a small hooked blade onto the end of a sturdy handle. He slips the blade over the base of dead canes and cuts them free from the plants with a single sweep. It means no bending over and cuts down on the time required to complete the annual pruning process.

After the old canes are removed, the fruit-bearing canes can be cut back to a comfortable picking height. If kept less than 1.5 metres tall, plants will require little in the way of support; otherwise they may have to be trained to a system of posts and wires to prevent canes breaking due to wind. Many gardeners tie up to seven canes together in bunches with pieces of twine or string. But this sometimes leads to problems with fungal infections amongst the tightly clustered foliage. The more open the canes are, the better the air circulation and the smaller the risk of disease.

Ken always cuts his canes back to chest level after pruning. "The Boyne variety produces strong and vigorous canes," he says, "and I find that they need no additional support at all if they're kept at this height."

Raspberry plants can produce a crop for many years if properly cared for. A dozen plants is usually sufficient for a family's requirements—enough to provide fresh raspberries to top breakfast cereal throughout the season, to create plenty of raspberry desserts, and to have raspberries on hand for freezing or for making jams and jellies. "I'm always amazed at how much fruit there is to harvest," says Ken. "I can pick morning and evening, at the peak of the season, and still just barely keep up with the ripening process. When I planted these canes a long time ago, I didn't realize what a tasty investment I was making for so many years to come!"

David and Susan Walker
Fredericton

David and Susan Walker live in a relatively new subdivision on the north side of Fredericton, where they have a lovely perennial border around the perimeter of the property behind the house. Susan is an accomplished gardener and David takes an interest in growing the trees and shrubs that dot their landscape. But David grew up on a farm and was always more interested in producing crops than in keeping a manicured landscape. So one day in 1983, while out jogging near abandoned fields in the neighborhood, he noticed some acreage that was flat with easy access from the street: perfect for growing strawberries. And that's all it took for the start of Sunset Strawberry U-Pick.

"There was a lot of trial and error when we first started growing strawberries," admits Susan. After they planted their first crop, she can remember spending long days and weeks in the berry patch down on her hands and knees, weeding. "Lamb's quarters grew in abundance," she confesses, as did a large variety of perennial weeds. They wanted to use minimum amounts of herbicide, but they also wanted to reduce the competition that weeds presented to their strawberry plants. So over the years, as they prepared new fields for planting, they devised a system whereby a broad spectrum herbicide was applied in the fall in order to have a weed-free field in which to begin planting the next spring. This means that Susan spends far less time on her hands and knees fighting with plants they don't want in their fields.

In addition to weed control, the Walkers have learned a great deal about their crop's productivity cycles. For example, strawberry plants only bear well for a few growing seasons. "Three harvests are ideal," says Susan, "although we have kept some plants in the field for as long as six years." Older strawberry plants tend to get an elongated crown, which impacts the amount and the size of fruit that can be harvested. And fields that have been in production for several years tend to get progressively more weedy. As a result, the Walkers established a planting rotation that has them putting in new strawberry plantlets each spring. They start as early as May 1 because their soil is sandy and workable early in the growing season. Growers with heavier loam have to wait a bit longer for the best planting conditions, but try to get their planting done as early in the year as possible in order to maximize the number of runners produced on the strawberries in the first season.

The Walkers use a machine that automatically spaces their plants at 45 cm intervals in the row, 1 m distances between the rows. "This is a good spacing for home gardeners to use," says Susan, who is always the person sitting on their planting machine, seeing that the bare-root, dormant strawberry plantlets are properly dropped into the soil. "Proper spacing means that there should be adequate room for runners to form and produce daughter plants."

Although a strawberry planter makes life simpler for large growers like the Walkers, there is some advantage to placing each plant in the ground by hand. "That way the plant's roots can be spread out over the ground surface in a circle around the crown," notes Susan. The crown is where a strawberry plant's leaves meet its roots; this is the part of the plant that shouldn't be buried too deep or allowed to remain too far out of the soil. "It's important to have the crown right at the soil surface," says Susan, "with the earth tamped gently all around it." When properly planted, newly-placed strawberry plants rapidly establish themselves.

After planting is completed, it's important for strawberries to be kept well watered. "We try to plant when a rain is in the forecast," says Susan. "Then 'mother nature' does the initial watering for us."

As soon as new strawberry plants begin to grow, they have a tendency to produce flowers. And although it's tempting to leave those in place the first year, it's much better to snip them off, to encourage the plant to produce runners. Runners are the long, thin stems that grow out from a mother strawberry to produce daughter plants, and are what provide the next year's harvest. "Runners will go anywhere, so we try to train them to grow within the row," says Susan. To encourage runner production, David applies a balanced fertilizer to the fields early in the growing season. "It's always a matter of balancing the amount of foliage and runner growth with the amount of flowering, especially with plants that have been in the ground for more than a year." Home gardeners can apply compost as a top dressing once

"There was a lot of trial and error when we first started growing strawberries." Fredericton's Susan Walker remembers long days spent weeding the berry patch.

in the spring and then a second time after plants have gone through a renovation process.

And what does "renovation" mean, with respect to strawberries? "We cut the leaves of the plants off with a mower, soon after harvest is complete," says Susan "and then David runs a tiller up the rows directly over top of the current year's mother plants." This causes the daughter plants to take over as mother plants, and results in a new burst of leaf, root, and runner growth. Unless a strawberry patch is renovated in this way, on an annual basis, fruit production will suffer and the plants will eventually degenerate.

After strawberry beds are renovated, sprayed for weeds and given additional fertilizer, they are left to grow until late in the fall, when they have to be prepared for winter. "We put a ten to twelve-centimetre layer of straw over the rows, just after Halloween each year," says Susan. They wait this late so that the ground is completely frozen and so that berry plants are dormant. The straw helps to keep the soil frozen during mild spells in the winter, so that plants don't get pushed up out of the ground with frost heaving; they remove the straw after the snow melts, during the first or second week of April. It's left between rows to act as a mulch for weed control, and to serve as a soft place to kneel during the harvest picking.

The Walkers spend many anxious days worrying about late spring frosts, after they've removed straw from their berry plants. "We have an irrigation system and can turn it on around 4 o'clock in the morning, if a frost is in the weather forecast," says Susan. "The water that sprays out over the berries may turn to ice, if it gets cold enough, but it'll buffer the temperature enough to keep the plants from being damaged." Home gardeners could cover their strawberry patch with a tarp or sheets of newspaper to provide the same level of spring protection.

The three weeks that it takes to get their crop picked each June are hectic ones for the Walkers. "It's sun-up to sun-down," says Susan, "except if it's a day that brings pouring rain." But she admits that harvest time is one of her favourite parts of the business. "People just love to pick our strawberries." Seniors often come in the morning, she says, "and they tell me that picking strawberries takes them back to their childhood." People who work all day arrive in the evenings. "They come to relax while picking, or they come on weekends and bring their children. We meet so many nice folks!"

Every year the Walkers plant more varieties in their fields. They've had great success with V-star, an early, sweet berry. But V-star is on the small side, and "people do like big berries," says Susan. The Walkers make a point of trying out new releases like Brunswick, Sable, and Cabot—just to see how they'll fare—but they always plant Honey-eye and Kent varieties, which are solid producers with good-sized fruit.

With all these strawberries at their disposal, what's the Walker's favourite strawberry recipe? "David is fond of strawberry pie, both the baked and glazed types," says Susan. But she's content with a fresh strawberry milkshake, every night after they close their U-pick. Sounds like a well-deserved treat after seeing little balls of red all day!

Daryl Hunter
Keswick Ridge

"Because my mother always made great apple pie and apple sauce," is Daryl Hunter's response, when asked the main reason for his intense and ongoing interest in apples. The other reason is that he fondly remembers going out for family drives and exploring old, abandoned orchards when he was a child. "We'd take a picnic and climb over rail fences to have lunch under the trees on Sunday afternoons in the summer."

When he and his wife, Joan, moved to their Keswick Ridge home in the mid-1970s, Daryl decided to grow the Yellow Transparent apples his mother had used to make all of those traditional Maritime desserts. He was living in apple country, after all, with dozens of commercial orchards within a 40-kilometre area, and knew he should be able to find a source for the tree. "But when I asked a neighbouring apple grower for seeds, I got a big surprise," he remembers with a chuckle. It was the first time he realized that apple trees aren't usually started directly from seed, and that all of the varieties he knew were propagated as clones by grafting. "That was my initiation into the world of apples." From there, Daryl learned how apples are grown in both large and small orchards. He planted trees in his own yard and experimented with ways to produce a crop without the need for disease and insect sprays. And he started to research the history of apple growing in New Brunswick. Today, there isn't much that he doesn't know about his favourite type of fruit. And yes, he does have his own Yellow Transparent apples for making pies.

Daryl grafted his first tree in 1977. Grafting starts with the removal of tissue from a desired variety, usually in the form of a stem which is referred to as "scion" wood. The scion will grow into the fruit bearing part of the apple tree. Scion wood is gathered from mature trees during the winter, when the tissue is completely dormant. It is kept in cold storage until it can be grafted on to a rootstock of some other variety, usually in March or April.

"Root stock" refers to the base of an apple tree, which includes the root system and part of the main trunk. It's winter hardy, and transmits other desirable traits to the scion, such as disease resistance or dwarfing tendencies. Some of the more common root stocks used to grow apple trees in New Brunswick's short seasons include Beautiful Arcade (originated in Russia), M 26, MM 111, and MM 106. The "M" refers to Malling, which is an apple research station in Britain. "MM" refers to Merton Malling, which is simply a different root-stock series released from the same British facility. These root stocks are started from seed but never grown to become fruit-bearing trees. Their entire reason for being is to support the growth of other varieties of apples. "McIntosh and Cortland are two varieties of apples that grow on grafted trees so that their genetic integrity is maintained," says Daryl. If an apple flower is pollinated by a bee, a variety of genes might be introduced in the pollen that is delivered to the blossom. These genes would then be in the seeds produced inside of the resulting apple. And if these seeds were used to grow new trees, a McIntosh would no longer be a McIntosh, and a Cortland would no longer be a Cortland, because of the different genes that they would contain. Grafting doesn't involve the mixing of genetic material from the flowers of two different parent trees, so grafted apple trees always remain true to variety.

In the years since his first grafting experiments, Daryl Hunter has melded together thousands of scions and root stocks. He has done much of this work on his own trees, grafting pieces of interesting varieties onto individual branches here and there. "I've had 65 trees to work with over the years," he says, "but

Daryl Hunter grafted his first apple tree in 1977. Since then, he has melded together hundreds of scions and root stocks.

I've grafted 135 varieties onto them." Not all of these trees and grafts are still living due to Daryl's yearly battle with deer, who love to nibble in his orchard; still, it's amazing to see how many cultivars remain. Daryl is most interested in heritage types of apples, which can't be found on supermarket shelves these days, but were commonly planted by our ancestors. Through grafting, he intends to archive as many of these old-fashioned cultivars as possible, in his own garden, to safeguard their genetic character. While some people collect stamps, Daryl collects apple trees.

Near the beginning of his archival efforts, Daryl became aware of the New Brunswick apple, which he describes as a "variety that was the fruit-breeding creation of Francis Peabody Sharp." Sharp developed New Brunswick's first commercial apple orchard in Woodstock, back in 1849, and went on to establish a nursery and a cider operation. By 1892, he had 1,600 varieties of hybrid apples under trial. One of them was the New Brunswick apple, commonly called the New Brunswicker, which has pale yellow fruit, striped with red, and which has firm flesh that's crisp but tender, juicy but tart. It's a great cooking apple, according to Daryl, and one that Sharp felt was "the first apple of quality that gave evidence of being completely adapted to New Brunswick." Homestead orchards throughout the province were planted with this variety, and some of those trees still exist. Other Sharp releases include Peabody Greening, Honey Pink, Woodstock Bloom, Fameuse, and Crimson Beauty; Daryl has most of these varieties on his own trees.

Along with learning about F.P. Sharp, Daryl has gathered information about planting, pruning, and fertilizing requirements for apples. He has learned about the insects that attack apple trees and has looked for organically-based control methods. All of this information—as well as a series of photographs and recipes—have been collated on a compact disc entitled *The Kitchen Orchard*, for sale locally and popular with home gardeners. It's an impressive effort for a person who didn't know much about apples until he went looking for a Yellow Transparent!

THE SECRETS OF GARDENING WITH FRUIT

- Remember to purchase both male and female kiwi plants if you want to have fruit to harvest.
- Protect both kiwi and grapes from late spring frosts, because they flower early and you'll lose your harvest if flowers are killed by cold temperatures.
- Plant all fruit-bearing plants in full sun in well-drained soil.
- Learn to prune or "renovate" fruit-bearing plants properly to ensure good harvests.
- Protect the roots of kiwi and grape plants in winter with a covering of evergreen boughs.
- Protect strawberries with a ten to twelve-centimetre layer of straw in the fall.
- Consider planting heritage varieties of apples in your garden, as many have exceptional disease and pest resistance.

FAVOURITE FRUIT RECIPES

Fruit Pizza with Kiwi

1 1/4 cups flour
1/2 cup sugar
2/3 cups softened margarine
250 g cream cheese, softened
1/3 cup icing sugar
1 tsp vanilla
fresh blueberries
fresh sliced strawberries
canned mandarin orange segments
kiwifruit, sliced
1/4 cup apricot or peach jam
1 tbsp water

Mix the flour, sugar and margarine until a ball is formed. Press into an ungreased 12-inch pizza pan, forming a rim around the edge. Bake on the centre rack of the oven at 350°F for about 12 minutes. Cool. Beat the cream cheese, the icing sugar and the vanilla together in a small bowl until smooth. Spread over cooled crust. Arrange the fruit in an attractive pattern over the cream cheese. Stir the jam and water together. Dab onto the fruit using a pastry brush. Chill. Serves 12.

Strawberry Salad

6 cups lettuce of mixed greens
1 1/2 cups crumbled feta cheese
1/2 cup slivered almonds, toasted
2 cups halved strawberries
pepper and salt

Dressing:
1 garlic clove, minced
1/2 tsp honey dijon mustard
2 tbsp raspberry vinegar
1 tbsp balsamic vinegar
1 tbsp brown sugar
1/4 cup vegetable oil

Mix greens with cheese, almonds and strawberries. Season with salt and pepper. Set aside. Mix the ingredients for the dressing until well blended. Pour over salad at serving time. Serves 6.

Peanut Butter Apple Crumble

This is a fifty-year-old recipe that was developed by Daryl Hunter's mother one day because she didn't have enough butter on hand to make her traditional apple crisp; she substituted peanut butter to make up the difference. Daryl recommends that tart cooking apples be used, such as Yellow Transparents, New Brunswickers, Crimson Beauty, Dudley Winters or Alexanders.

6 medium cooking apples
1/2 cup flour
1/2 cup sugar
3 tbsp butter

3 tbsp peanut butter
1/4 tsp salt
nutmeg or cinnamon to taste
  (optional)

Prepare the apples by peeling and slicing them into a shallow buttered dish approximately six by ten inches. If you want a juicier crumble add 1/2 cup of water to the dish. If the apples are very tart, dissolve a tablespoon or two of sugar into this water before pouring it over them into the dish. Another option is to add a pinch of cinnamon or nutmeg to the sugar/water mixture, for flavour.

Prepare the crumble by combining nutmeg, sugar, flour and salt in a bowl and mixing well. Cut the peanut butter and butter into this mixture. Sprinkle over the apples. Bake in a 350°F oven for about 35 minutes or until golden brown. Serve plain, with cereal cream or with vanilla ice cream. Serves 6.

Grape Jelly

3 qts blue grapes
1/2 cup water

7 cups sugar
1 pouch liquid pectin (Certo)

Stem and thoroughly crush the grapes. Add the water and bring to a boil. Simmer, covered, for ten minutes. Extract the juice by straining through a jelly bag (made from muslin or cotton). Place the juice (you should have four cups) in an 8-quart saucepan and add the sugar. Bring to a rolling boil, stirring constantly. Stir in the liquid pectin and continue to stir over high heat until the mixture comes to a boil again. Boil hard for 1 minute stirring constantly. Remove from the heat, and skim off any surface foam. Pour quickly into sterilized jars, seal with flaps, and screw rings on tightly. Makes 6 1/2 cups of jelly.

Ted Wiggans, Frog Lake

VEGETABLES

"A gardener's work is never at an end: it begins with the year, and continues to the next: he prepares the ground, and then he sows it; after that he plants, and then he gathers the fruits."

John Evelyn, 1706

Through the long months of late fall and winter, when my New Brunswick garden is frozen solid and covered with many feet of snow, I am obliged, like many other Canadians, to rely on supermarket produce for fresh vegetables. Somehow, only a few weeks after it becomes impossible to pick fresh greens, tomatoes, and cucumbers for a suppertime salad, or pull ears of corn off the stalks, beets from the ground, or green beans off the vine, I find myself longing for spring so I can have the luxury of preparing a meal with food picked fresh, just minutes earlier. In the summer we take for granted the many vegetables at our disposal, and we almost get bored with them. But when the end of the growing season comes, it's a shock to realize how long we'll have to wait until things will be growing again.

My vegetable garden is about half an acre, and it provides more than enough harvest for our family of five. Over the years, I've experimented with many different ways of growing things, but in recent years, I find myself using the same methods over and over because they work best for me. I used to practice wide-row planting, for example, but discovered that a single line of carrots, beets, or onions means I can get the hoe right up against the plant base to keep in-row weeds at bay. A wide row with more than one plant (across) means weeding on my hands and knees—I'm just not talented enough with a hoe to get in between plants without cutting something off in the process!

I always put cucumbers next to corn, because by the time the cucumbers start running, the corn is at least 25 cm high and can cope with this company running around the base of its stalks. I put individual seed potatoes in a trench, then cover them over with more and more soil as the summer progresses, so that by the end of the season they are nicely hilled up. Potatoes that don't have enough soil covering them tend to get sunburned and develop green skins (and green-skinned potatoes can make you sick). I always sow a second crop of beets about a month after the first planting session; that way we have beet greens for a longer period of time, which are the only part of a beet worth eating, according to my children. And I always put romaine lettuce transplants between broccoli seedlings because the lettuce is ready for harvest within a month, and, once removed, there's lots of room for the broccoli to spread out.

I try to use a 'companion planting' approach because I've learned, over the years, that one variety always does better if it's planted beside certain other varieties. There is not always scientific proof for most of these combinations, but they really seem to work. Sometimes it's because one plant keeps pests or diseases away from another; other times it's because one plant enhances the growth of another. I always put marigolds between my tomatoes, peppers, and broccoli, because marigolds keep pests away from those vegetables. Celery planted between each of the bean poles helps to keep rust and fungus from infecting the beans. I plant an onion at 25 cm intervals along a row of carrots, because the smell of onion helps to mask the smell of the carrots, which confuses the carrot rust fly. Radish, which attract flea beetles, are planted with cucumbers—better a flea-bitten radish than no cucumbers! And some plants should definitely be kept apart. For example, I keep sunflowers away from the potatoes, and never put tomatoes beside the asparagus bed. I also find that carrots shouldn't be near dill, and potatoes should be kept away from pumpkins. You'll find a helpful companion planting guide at the end of this chapter.

My own vegetables are fertilized with nothing but compost. A member of the Fredericton Backyard Compost Committee, I've been an avid composter for more than twenty years. But I can't create enough compost to meet the needs of all of my gardens. So I also use composted chicken manure, with great results. Many gardeners swear by well-rotted manure from neighbourhood farmers, but unless a manure has been through a hot composting process, it's bound to be full of weed seeds, no matter how long it's been since it came out of the animal. I can remember adding lots of old cow manure to my first garden because I was determined to grow everything organically, and I'd never been told that some weed seeds can remain viable—even after passing through the stomach of a cow or horse, and even after being in a manure pile for twenty odd years. What a nightmare! For several years it seemed like I was harvesting nothing but weeds.

The rewards of vegetable gardening are many. The following gardeners are experts at growing food for themselves and others, with lots of good advice.

Ted Wiggans
Frog Lake

When Ted Wiggans started looking for a piece of property on which to start a farm, he travelled to some interesting areas of New Brunswick. But it wasn't until he came upon a location at the end of a long country lane, overlooking rolling hills, lush meadows, and a small lake, that he knew his search was over. He'd have 57 acres of ground to work with: a few acres of wetland and woods, with the rest consisting of pastureland and a number of hay fields, each field surrounded by hedgerows that marked the farming practices of an earlier era. The Wiggans family moved into a house built in 1864, restoring it and constructing a greenhouse. They began to cultivate the earth, acquiring some sheep and, finally, a fitting name for their new home: The Shepherd's Garden, a farm that produces lamb, wool, and vegetables. Today, in a picturesque setting near Frog Lake, New Brunswick, the Wiggans family have a large market garden that flourishes with a shepherd's touch.

The Shepherd's Garden is an organic farm. Registered with the Maritime Certified Organic Grower's Cooperative, the family follows a strict set of production processes to meet yearly inspection requirements. Their aim—and result—is a farm where soil fertility is optimized to provide a balanced nutrient supply that supports both animal and plant life, using a balance of pest, disease, and weed management techniques, with proper crop selection and rotation. An organic approach to agriculture is one that sustains a harmonious partnership with the environment.

The vegetable crop from The Shepherd's Garden is destined for sale at the Boyce Farmer's Market in Fredericton each Saturday morning, but production begins well in advance of harvest. To get a jump on the growing season, Ted starts seeds of various vegetables and herbs in his large greenhouse in late winter. These seeds are sown into "soil blocks"—created by using a special tool designed to make several cubes of soil mix at one time, to fit into seeding trays or flats. The soil mix that Ted prefers to use consists of one part composted sheep manure, four parts peat moss, one part topsoil, and a bit of lime; it's a modification of one recommended by Eliot Coleman in his book *The New Organic Grower—A Master's Manual of Tools and Techniques for the Home and Market Gardener*. Ted recommends this helpful guide to anyone interested in organic gardening.

When his seedlings are sufficiently mature, Ted either transplants them into ground that's covered by the greenhouse or—if frost season has passed—directly into the garden. Here, they're sometimes placed in rows that have been covered with a black plastic mulch. This type of cover serves a dual purpose: it helps to warm the soil, and it keeps weeds from growing around the base of plants.

Speaking of weeds, it seems that there is never an end to the chore of keeping them from overtaking the crop at The Shepherd's Garden. Hoeing, hand weeding, and mulching are permitted organic practices. Ted also rotates areas of the garden into non-production phases, planted with buckwheat or winter rye—both of which grow so vigorously that they effectively choke out weeds, in addition to adding nutrients to the soil when they're plowed under. Ted also recommends oil seed radish as a cover crop; not only do these types of radish help to break the weed cycle, but their large roots help to break up heavy soil. He plants these late in the growing season so they'll be killed by frost before going to seed.

Organic agriculture aims at minimizing loss caused by disease and pests. Ted selects varieties that have natural resistance and often plants around the life cycle of certain insects. He uses "Bt" (*Bacillus thuringiensis*), a natural pesticide for cole crops like broccoli and cabbage, and he plants a large garlic crop, which repels insects. But he finds that his best tool against bug infestations is to have strong, healthy plants that can ward off pest attacks all by themselves.

All through the summer, crops of lettuce, spinach, mesculin, swiss chard, and beets grow in large planting beds at The Shepherd's Garden. It's a place where beans and tomatoes and peppers and onions mature in rich, fertile soil, a place where sheep roam contentedly across the pasture. The Wiggans family successfully shepherd their land, growing healthy, organic food for New Brunswickers.

Ted Wiggans in The Shepherd's Garden, an organic farm that produces lamb, wool, and vegetables.

Peter and Marilyn Cronk
North Head, Grand Manan

Peter and Marilyn Cronk grow vegetables and herbs in an idyllic setting on Grand Manan Island, off New Brunswick's southern coast. Ocean waves roll onto the beach at nearby Whale Cove; from overhead comes the raucous call of seagulls. In the salt marsh behind the house, great blue herons swoop and rest, along with other nesting waterfowl. Growing in hedgerows and meadows that surround the property are native wildflowers and shrubs—lupins, daisies, fireweed, raspberries, red osier dogwood, and virgin's bower.

Added to the beauty of the setting is the Bay of Fundy's buffering effect on the Grand Manan climate. Less-than-extreme winter temperatures and limited snowfall allow the island to fall into hardiness Zone 5 or 6, while ocean mists and fog provide high humidity levels and respite from periods of drought.

Even with the aesthetics of these surroundings and the value of a moderate climate, gardening in the middle of the Bay of Fundy still has its challenges, including an occasional hurricane. And Peter and Marilyn have tackled just about every imaginable situation during their years as Island gardeners.

When they first started gardening in the late 1970s, the Cronks planted an apple orchard and a strawberry U-Pick. They were determined to grow these crops organically to guarantee harvests free of chemical pesticides. But the apples they started with were McIntosh and Cortland varieties, both prone to disease and insect attacks. And their five thousand strawberries took a tremendous amount of hand weeding, because that's just about the only way to grow these without using herbicides. They eventually fixed their orchard problems by switching to more disease-resistant varieties of Liberty, Freedom, and Red Free apples, and they eliminated the time-consuming and back-breaking job of weeding long rows of strawberries by tilling up the entire patch. On its newly-turned soil they decided to start a market garden. It turned out to be the right time for them to be converting to vegetables and herbs: a farmer's

Being close to the seashore means that Peter and Marilyn Cronk have ready access to seaweed, which they often add to their compost pile.

market had just opened on the Island, giving them a captive audience for their produce.

Growing anything organically means taking extra measures to keep soil as healthy as possible. For their own shallow soil, the Cronks make annual applications of organically-derived nutrients such as compost, bone meal, blood meal, and fish meal. Being close to the seashore means they have ready access to seaweed, and they often collect large amounts after storms or high tides have thrown it up on the beach, adding it to the compost pile. In the fall, they usually spread thick layers of rockweed over their planting beds, then till it into the soil the following spring.

Like most organic gardeners, the Cronks are actively involved in crop rotation. Each year, a portion of their land is taken out of production and sown with a green manure crop (such as annual rye, or buckwheat). If thickly sown, a cover crop helps to choke out weeds, and adds organic matter to soil when tilled in at the end of the growing season. Planting cover crops is a standard approach to organic agriculture—but not so standard is the Cronks's practice of adding sunflower seeds to the rye and buckwheat at planting time. When they begin to flower, the sunflowers add colour to a green field, "and the birds like it too," says Marilyn, recalling the many blue jays and chickadees attracted to their fields when the sunflowers go to seed.

Once, when Peter was experimenting with sources of organic fertilizer, he thought seashells might be a way to add more calcium to the soil. So he spread one of his fields with intact scallop shells and then tried to till them into the ground. "It wasn't such a good idea," he admits, recalling the difficulties he had in getting the shells to break down. "It would have been better to have crushed them first," he chuckles, pointing out a large piece of shell still lying on the soil, years after this experiment.

The Cronk's largest vegetable gardens are planted with typical species like beets, carrots, potatoes, broccoli, beans, zucchini, squash, and cucumber. Not so typical, however, are things they've had to deal with because they're gardening on an island, surrounded by natural areas full of wildlife. Take floating row cover, for example. Many organic growers use a system of laying Remay over a row after it has been planted, anchoring its edges and ends with soil. Remay is a thin, linen-like fabric that allows sunlight—but not insects—to penetrate. It expands or "floats" upwards as the crop below it matures. Peter thought this would be a good way to protect some of his crops from pests, so went to the expense of purchasing it at the beginning of one gardening season. Although Remay is supposed to last for several years (thus worth the initial expense), Peter didn't have to worry about storing the product from one season to another. "It blew away shortly after it was installed the first year," he confesses…one of the hazards of gardening with ocean breezes.

The Cronks also have to deal with unwelcome visitors to their garden. Muskrats live in the marsh behind the house, and, to keep them from totally devouring his carrots, Peter covered parts of the garden with mesh. "It's recycled fish net," he says "and we have lots of that around here." The netting has a one-inch mesh, which seems to be a tight-enough weave to keep muskrats from getting through.

To control the many pheasants that live in surrounding woods and fields, the Cronks have had to be imaginative. They planted all lettuce and herbs (gourmet food to a pheasant!) in raised beds made from recycled railway ties, and completely covered the beds in chicken wire, which is held in place with old herring stakes. "These stakes are stronger than bamboo," describes Peter, "which is important when it comes to standing up to the weight and will of full-sized, hungry pheasants."

Then there are the larger garden invaders. "Grand Manan has the highest density of deer anywhere in the province," says Peter. "You can see them most evenings in the field across the road." Deer are difficult to discourage once they target a particular garden, but some gardeners find that hair or urine spread around the garden seems to act as a good deterrent. "I tend to consolidate the crops that deer like to eat—such as beet greens and lettuce—by planting them in one place in the garden. I put sheep fencing around the whole thing but fix it to temporary posts, so I can shift it around the garden as I rotate the location of the crops each year." Peter finds this approach effective, even though the fence is only four feet high and not too sturdy, because there are so many other places in the neighbourhood that the deer can move on to, gardens that take less effort to raid. Are they lazy deer, or just choosy? Whatever the answer, fencing seems to be enough of a deterrent to keep them from filling up at the Cronks.

Even with all this wildlife and weather, Peter and Marilyn reap profitable harvests from their large garden. They sell at the farmer's market on Saturdays, and directly to island residents and tourists the rest of the week. They also deliver produce regularly to island restaurants, and provide chefs with fresh herbs. Without question, their biggest crop of the summer is sweet basil, which they start in their lean-to greenhouse beside the garage and transplant to the garden after soil has warmed up in late spring. "I mulch it with black plastic" says Peter. The plastic not only controls weeds, but helps to keep soil warm through the cool island nights—basil needs lots of heat to grow well.

So, with the climate on their side, with good soil husbandry part of their normal routine, and with the willingness to co-exist with wildlife both feathered and furry, the Cronks continue growing vegetables on Grand Manan. It's a great life!

Thea Visbach
Prince William

There are many ways to grow vegetables, but for Thea Visbach, the method was determined by two things. When she and husband Fritz moved into their retirement home in Prince William, just west of Fredericton, she wanted to make the vegetable patch easy to access from the house, and of a design that didn't require much bending or kneeling. She also knew that the most suitable, sunny spot on the property was in a bit of a depression where water tended to collect each spring, and where soil was unusually cold and compacted until late in the season. That meant she would always have to wait for the area to get warm and dry each year before she could begin tilling and planting. All these factors convinced her that building a series of raised beds would be a good way to grow vegetables.

These raised beds could be constructed in the preferred sunny location because their planting surface would be elevated above the wet ground. Their chosen height and width meant that she and Fritz wouldn't have to kneel down or bend over too far to plant and cultivate. And raised beds are known for being particularly effective for growing vegetables because they aren't designed to allow those flat walking areas between plants—with beds, gardeners typically lean across from one side or another when planting or weeding, so soil never gets compacted. For Thea's purposes, the whole idea of raised beds seemed perfect. Her idea became a reality, and results were more than satisfactory. Other than pole beans and peas, which she needs to grow on support systems and so plants outside of the structure, the Visbach's raised-bed vegetable garden has been a rewarding success.

Growing her own food is important for Thea. "You know what you're eating when you pick it from your own garden." And she says this based on years of experience. Both she and Fritz were trained in horticulture, operating a florist and nursery for many years after emigrating to Canada from Holland. "Having a vegetable garden was always second nature to us," she confesses, "although it was originally much larger and planted directly in the ground." But after their retirement, and then after Fritz passed away, raised beds were much more practical for garden size and maintenance. "I can water it easily during these hot summers we've been having, because all of the plants are close together," says Thea. Actually, the plants in a raised bed usually need to be watered a bit less often than those in a garden planted directly in the ground, because bed plants grow so quickly that their leaves touch and shade the soil below from moisture loss.

Thea constructed her raised beds from cedar logs resting in four tiers in a rectangle. She filled the base of the structure with topsoil but mixed a combination of chicken manure, peat moss, vermiculite, and mushroom compost into the top layer to make the medium more friable and rich in organic matter. Over the summers since her beds were first built, the topsoil has tended to sink a bit, so Thea tops it up with peat-based potting soil that she buys from a garden centre. "I blend it in well, with the medium that is already there," she adds, " so that there is uniformity in the plants' root zone." She also works in compost and manure each season to replenish any lost nutrients.

Thea plants her raised beds intensively; by the end of the summer, they're a lush canopy of green. She grows kale and endive, both favourite vegetables in her native Holland. She also grows leeks, which she starts early indoors in her greenhouse, then transplants to the raised beds at the start of the gardening season. And she's always pleased with how long and straight her carrots are. "They have lots of soil depth to grow into," she says, "and they don't run into restrictions like stones or compacted soil layers that often cause carrots to become crooked or stunted." She puts tomato plants at the corners of the beds, planting cucumbers and squash around the edges so they can trail over the sides. At the beginning of the

By planting her vegetable garden in raised beds, Thea Visbach can avoid kneeling and bending in order to plant and cultivate.

season, she mulches the tops of the soil in the beds with thick layers of moist newspapers; these keep weed seeds from blowing in, and they also help to retain soil moisture. Crops like radishes and beans are picked when fully mature; Thea then removes these plants so she can sow a second crop for late summer harvest.

Growing vegetables is just a small part of what Thea does well. A regular judge of horticulture competitions at the Fredericton Exhibition, she also conducts dried flower workshops and seminars upon special request. She has a large perennial garden, and an annual hanging basket and planter display that's the envy of anyone who sees it. But she'll always be partial to gardening with vegetables. "It's their freshness," she exclaims. "Nothing can beat growing your own!"

The Secrets of Gardening with Vegetables

- Keep your soil healthy by adding compost or composted manures to build up its organic matter content.
- Mulch with black plastic or thick layers of moist newspaper to warm the soil, keep weeds under control, and retain moisture.
- Rotate crops around the garden so that disease and insects don't build up in any one spot.
- Sow green manure crops like annual rye or buckwheat, and till them in to add organic matter to the soil.
- Protect crops from animals using mesh or wire fencing.
- Use floating row cover for insect control, but anchor it well to keep it from being blown away.
- Deter deer by sprinkling urine or hair around your garden.
- Consider raised beds if you have a wet site, or if you want to reduce bending and kneeling.
- Choose disease- and insect-resistant varieties so there is less need for pesticides.
- Train cucumber and squash to grow over the edges of raised beds to conserve space and to make for easy picking.

Companion Planting

Vegetable	'Likes'	'Dislikes'
asparagus	tomatoes, parsley, basil	
beans	potatoes, carrots, cucumbers	onion, garlic
pole beans	celery, corn, summer savory, lovage	onions, beets, kohlrabi, broccoli

Vegetable	'Likes'	'Dislikes'
carrots	beans, peas, onions, sage, tomatoes	dill
corn	potatoes, peas, cucumbers, pumpkin, squash	
cucumbers	beans, corn, peas, radishes, sunflowers	
potatoes	horseradish, marigolds, flax	fennel
tomatoes	marigolds, basil, beebalm	rue
broccoli	marigolds, nasturtiums, potatoes, beets, onions	strawberries, tomatoes, pole beans

Favourite Vegetable Recipes

Garden Vegetable Stuffing for Salmon

2 onions, chopped
1/4 cup butter or margarine
2 cups dry bread cubes
1 cup coarsely shredded carrot
1 cup cut-up fresh mushrooms
1/2 cup snipped fresh parsley
 (or 1 tbsp dried)
1 1/2 tbsp lemon juice
1 egg
1 clove garlic minced
2 teaspoons salt
1/4 tsp marjoram
1/4 tsp pepper

Cook and stir onion in butter until tender. Lightly mix in remaining ingredients. Place a cleaned 8 to 10 pound salmon in a large, greased baking dish and add stuffing to the cavity of the fish. Lay lemon slices on top of the fish. Cover the baking dish with foil and place in a 350° F oven for approximately 50 minutes, or until the fish flakes easily with a fork.

Curried Carrot Soup

1/4 cup butter
1 chopped onion
3 tsp curry
4 cups water

4 chicken bouillon cubes
8 large carrots chopped
1 tbsp sherry

Melt the butter and sauté onions until tender. Add water, curry, bouillon cubes, and carrots. Cook twenty minutes until carrots are soft. Purée in blender and reheat. Add sherry just before serving.

Broccoli Salad

1 head broccoli
1 head cauliflower
1 small onion, chopped fine
1/2 lb bacon, fried crisp

1/4 lb grated cheddar cheese
1/2 cup mayonnaise
1/2 cup sugar
2 tbsp vinegar

Cut the tips of the florets from the heads of broccoli and cauliflower. Mix the two vegetables together and add the onion, bacon, and cheese. In a separate bowl, mix the mayonnaise, sugar, and vinegar until smooth. Add to the rest of the ingredients, just before serving, and mix until the broccoli and cauliflower are completely coated.

Asparagus and New Potato Salad with Sugar Snap Peas

10 small new potatoes
3 tablespoons olive oil
12 asparagus spears
6 oz sugar snap peas
6 green onions chopped
1 tbsp red wine vinegar

2 tsp fresh thyme (or 1/2 tsp dried)
1/2 cup garlic mayonnaise
2 tsp Dijon mustard
2 tsp lemon juice

Scrub potatoes and boil until just tender. Drain. Transfer to a large serving dish and add green onions and 2 tablespoons of the olive oil. Season with salt and pepper to taste. Trim the ends from the asparagus and cut into pieces. Steam or microwave until just tender. Remove strings from the pea pods and steam or microwave until tender also. Add peas and asparagus to the potatoes. Mix the remaining 1 tablespoon of olive oil with the wine vinegar and the thyme. Pour over the vegetables and toss until they are coated. Let cool to room temperature. Stir mustard and lemon juice into the mayonnaise and serve this with the salad.

Howard Erb and Marilyn LaFrance, Cambridge

Herbs

"A herb is a plant that has fragrance, flavoring, or medicinal value"
Susan McClure

I distinctly remember the gardens that my mother and grandfather planted in the summers of my childhood. My mother's garden was large for an urban setting, and was intended to grow enough vegetables for canning and freezing to support a family of six all through the winter. My grandfather's was even bigger, as he was a New Brunswick farmer growing things for sale at a roadside stand.

In all the seasons that I spent weeding and harvesting both of those gardens, I can only recall the presence of two types of herbs. There was always enough dill to make pickles with, and enough sage so that Sunday-dinner chickens and turkeys could be properly stuffed. Never would I have found a basil or rosemary plant. Not a single row would have been devoted to lovage or lemon balm. There wasn't even a clump of parsley. But that wasn't unusual for a typical New Brunswick garden of the day; gardening meant growing food, not fancy. I'd never heard of herbal tea (just Orange Pekoe) and I was accustomed to flavouring my food with salt and pepper.

Despite this introduction, the gardens I cultivate today are full of herbs. Over the past twenty years I have advanced from planting single patches of dill and sage to having a special "kitchen garden" entirely dedicated to culinary herbs. I have a collection of herbs for making teas and fragrant potpourri, and I grow a variety of herbs as "companion plants"—their job is to keep insect pests at bay.

I've learned which herbs are grown as annuals and which as perennials, hardy enough to survive cold Canadian winters. I've experimented with herbs in my family's food and am pleased to say that my children will happily consume cheese scones rich with thyme, roast pork smothered with marjoram, chicken barbequed with rosemary and omelettes full of parsley and chives. They love basil and garlic in bruschetta, and lemon balm or mint added to fruit salad. (Granted, they still question the value of adding lovage to a salad and the need to put lavender blossoms in shortbread cookies, but they'll get there!)

I've found herbs to be easy to grow. Generally speaking, they do best in the sunniest spot in the garden, in well-drained soil. They won't require much fertilizer because excess nutrients can reduce the plants' production of essential oils, making them less flavourful or fragrant. An application of compost around the base of perennial herbs each spring, or a monthly dose of manure tea for annual herbs, will usually suffice.

I'm not alone in my current passion for gardening with herbs. All around New Brunswick, hobby gardeners are planting and enjoying herbs. Restaurants are serving foods flavoured with fresh, local herbs. Farmer's markets and garden centres are devoting lots of shelf space to pots of herbs and herb seeds. And the story and secrets of gardening and using herbs is being told by several adventurous herb lovers.

Howard Erb and Marilyn LaFrance
H. Erb's Herbs, Cambridge

Marilyn LaFrance and her husband, Howard Erb, had a casual involvement with herbs up until a few years ago. That's when Howard retired and the couple moved back to Cambridge Narrows, an area of southern New Brunswick where past generations of his family had farmed. Both avid gardeners, the couple started out with a small greenhouse and a few planting beds, and decided to try growing herbs for sale to neighbours and friends…just as a hobby. But news of their venture quickly spread, and soon a second greenhouse was required to keep up with the demand, and more garden area was turned over to planting beds. They called their newly established business "H. Erb's Herbs."

It wasn't long before they had a market for fresh-cut herbs in restaurants in Saint John, and sufficient interest in potted herbs to expand their varieties. As business increased, Marilyn and Howard began to create unique "herbal gift gardens" in patio pots of various sizes; these were popular with customers who wanted to keep a few herbs growing on their window ledges or decks. They sold kits for making "basil beer bread," as well as unique dried herb mixtures, tomato-basil salads, pesto, and packets of fresh-cut herbs at farmer's markets in nearby Jemseg. At gardening clubs, senior's groups, and horticulture shows, they started giving talks about growing and using herbs. They acquired an organic certification for their farm, and prepared carefully-labelled display gardens that visitors are welcome to stroll through. "We've had a nice opportunity to meet people who come to tour the gardens," says Howard; from the start, they've had visitors from across Canada and Europe. Each guest is treated to the smells and tastes of the farm's bounty, and goes home with a pot or freshly-cut packet of herbs, because Howard insists that "there's room for herbs in everyone's life!"

In 1999 Howard and Marilyn planted 4,300 transplants into new production beds, spacing rows so they could accommodate a tractor-run cultivator to control weeds. Many of these plants were basil; the couple grow ten varieties of this heat-loving herb,

Marilyn LaFrance and Howard Erb began with a small greenhouse and a few planting beds…but news of their venture quickly spread.

which can't be set in the garden until the soil has really warmed up. According to Howard, the easiest type of basil for the hobby gardener is sweet basil, and he recommends sowing it directly into the soil in a sunny, well-drained garden location. Once it starts growing vigorously, flowers should always be pinched from the plant to encourage new growth. He and Marilyn both suggest harvesting basil (or any herb, for that matter) in mid-morning, just after dew has dried from leaves, while the plants' aromatic oils are at their most intense. Howard also recommends that a first-time herb grower try planting a bit of summer savory; it's a prolific producer and easily grown from seed sown directly in the garden at the start of the growing season. That Thanksgiving bird will taste all the better with home-grown savory in the dressing!

Also included in their new production beds was lovage, Marilyn's favourite. She finds it easy to grow but recommends giving it a few applications of compost tea through the growing season, as it's such a heavy feeder. Rather than keeping seed heads off her plants, she lets them mature and allows them to sow themselves in the garden so that she has lots of new seedlings to transplant each spring.

A cold February morning will find Howard and Marilyn planning a seed order for the coming season. Each year they add a few new varieties to their list, but still have less to order, because they've started to collect their own seeds in the fall. Their whole lives have become focused on herbs; a retirement hobby turning into a rewarding new career. And herbs, notes Howard, "have renewed my interest in food." Basil, one of their most popular herbs, finds its way into their versatile recipe for Pesto:

Pesto *(makes 3/4 to 1 cup)*

2 cups lightly packed, fresh basil leaves
1/4 cup fresh Italian (flat-leaf) parsley
1/4 cup pine nuts, roasted
2 cloves garlic, peeled
1/3 cup grated Parmesan cheese*
1/2 tsp salt
1/2 cup olive oil
1 tbsp butter

*If you are going to freeze pesto, add Parmesan cheese just before serving, as cheese doesn't freeze well.

Place all the ingredients in a blender. Purée until the sauce is smooth, pushing down the basil leaves as necessary. When you use this sauce on pasta, reserve 1/4 cup of the pasta's cooking water just before draining. Add all or part of this water to the pesto and drained pasta, until a desirable consistency is reached.

Pesto may be refrigerated for a week, but should be covered with a thin film of olive oil to prevent discolouration. It can also be frozen in ice cube trays.

Use pesto on pasta, pizza, bruschetta, beans, potatoes, or in minestrone soup.

Marinated Tomato Slices with Fresh Basil *(serves 4 to 6)*

2 large, ripe tomatoes
2 tbsp chopped fresh basil leaves
3 tbsp salad or olive oil
2 tbsp lemon juice
1/2 tsp salt
1/8 tsp freshly ground pepper
1/2 tsp sugar

Slice the tomatoes into a deep dish or glass pie plate. Sprinkle the tomato slices with the chopped basil. Mix remaining ingredients with a wire whisk or fork, and pour this dressing over the tomatoes. Marinate for at least 1 hour at room temperature, occasionally spooning the dressing over the tomatoes. Serve at room temperature or chilled.

Aaron and Anna Randall
Sweet Valley Herbs
Mouth of Keswick

In 1997, after a decade of experience as a chef in New Brunswick, Aaron Randall was becoming increasingly frustrated with the difficulty of finding local sources of fresh herbs. That's when he and his wife, Anna, decided to build a small greenhouse in which they could at least grow basil and rosemary. By trial and error, and with excellent assistance from Halifax Seed Company (a regional greenhouse supplier) they erected a small, plastic-covered, hoop-framed structure on their property in Mouth of Keswick, near Burtt's Corner, New Brunswick. That first year, they ordered seed and plants from Richters Herbs in Ontario, and learned about ways to propagate and harvest their initial crop. Their efforts were so successful that they decided to expand the operation, increasing the size of their greenhouse to a planting area of fifteen hundred square feet, and naming their business "Sweet Valley Herbs."

In the beginning, the Randalls quickly learned that growing herbs for commercial sale is "all about timing." Eventually they worked out a seeding schedule, whereby they always had four

Surprised by success: Anna and Aaron Randall's Sweet Valley Herbs.

The Randalls also discovered that it takes a long time for rosemary to germinate, and that they prefer certain varieties over others for fresh material. Their rosemary plants are now kept in large pots with several inches of gravel lining the bottoms, for drainage. They have huge stock plants from which they start cuttings on a regular basis. And Aaron finds that rosemary grows best if allowed to dry out between waterings.

Large, rectangular planters rest directly on the Randalls's greenhouse floor. Filled with a mixture of soil, composted fish manure, and peat moss, these planters hold sage, thyme, and oregano. Because of the box's volume, these perennial species should thrive for extended periods. Other production beds on the property contain large plantings of tarragon, chives, and mint. The tarragon isn't hardy and must be brought indoors during New Brunswick winters. The mint, which can be a terrible spreader, is allowed to ramble over a large growing area designated just for this species. The chives are cut back just as they begin to blossom, to keep them producing quantities of fresh, new shoots.

The Randalls sell their fresh herbs directly to restaurants in the Fredericton area and to a local wholesaler. They also take potted herbs, herbal vinegars, pesto, and herbal oils to Fredericton's Boyce Farmer's Market each Saturday morning. These market sessions are an opportunity to exchange news and information about using and growing herbs with their customers. They've also received heirloom recipes, which they encourage others to try and treasure for themselves. Here's an example:

Basil Cheddar Crisps

1 cup grated cheddar cheese
1/2 cup margarine
1/2 tsp Tabasco sauce
1 tsp prepared mustard

1 cup flour
2 to 6 tbsp chopped, fresh basil
1 1/2 cups rice crisp cereal

different ages of basil growing in the greenhouse. Beginning with seedlings in plug trays, and ending with plants growing in four-to-six-inch pots, they were able to ensure a continuous basil crop for harvesting through the summer. They consider basil to be the "king of herbs" and keep approximately four thousand basil plants, in various stages of development, all through the growing season.

Preheat oven to 350° C. In a large bowl, mix cheese, butter, Tabasco and mustard. Blend in flour and basil. Stir in cereal. Blend carefully and shape into balls. Place on greased cookie sheet and flatten with the bottom of a floured glass. Bake 15 minutes.

The Randalls consider basil to be the "king of herbs," and they keep four thousand basil plants all through the growing season.

Valerie Marr, King's Landing Historical Settlement, Prince William

Herbalist Valerie Marr is an important member of her community at King's Landing, New Brunswick. Respected by her neighbours as being wise in the world of medicine, known for her skills as a midwife, and admired for her healing teas and poultices, Valerie would be one of the first people called upon in the event of a mishap or accident in the local countryside—but only if this was the nineteenth century. King's Landing is not a real town or village. About 40 kilometres west of Fredericton, it's a historical settlement depicting life in New Brunswick in the 1800s. And Valerie plays the part of the Settlement's herbalist, showing modern visitors how things were done more than a century ago.

Valerie has been at King's Landing for 22 years. She first learned how herbs were important to New Brunswick's early settlers while researching plants that could be used as natural dyes. She discovered that, during the era depicted at King's Landing, herbs were used most often for medicine. Because doctors were few and far between, there was always a woman of the community who learned—either from her mother or from the native Maliseet and Mi'kmaq—about the use of plants for preventing or curing sickness. This woman was called a herbalist. She also learned about the settlers' culinary uses of herbs. Because there was no refrigeration in those times, there was often a great amount of spoilage. Herbs were added to some foods (especially meats) just as they were beginning to spoil, to mask the rotten taste.

Valerie explains that each King's Landing settler would have brought with them seeds, roots, or cuttings of favourite herbs. They would have tucked these materials into their settler's "kit," along with the other supplies, to set up a home in their adopted land. And if it came down to having to make a choice between fitting in a piece of furniture or having sufficient herbs among their travelling gear to help them start a garden, you can be sure that the plants would have won out for space.

Working in one century and living in another makes her Valerie's life unique. She starts each day at King's Landing by selecting a period costume that will suit the various aspects of her role as the Settlement's herbalist. "Some days I work in the herb garden behind the Morehouse home," she says, "so I wear exactly what a woman might have worn to do garden chores." Other days she dons a fancy bonnet and finer clothes and takes a stroll to catch up on local gossip or to read tea leaves. In all of this activity, she interacts with the visiting public, showing them how to collect and dry herbs from the garden, or how to make teas, decoctions, ointments, lineaments, poultices, and herbal pillows. She also makes sure that labelled, historically-appropriate herbs such as horseradish, sage, elecampane, thyme, oregano, tarragon, and sorrel are hanging from hearths in Settlement homes.

All this work keeps herbal knowledge of the past alive in the present, but Valerie doesn't recommend that a person go out and start grazing on medicinal herbs indiscriminately. Just because a herb is a natural thing, she cautions, doesn't mean that it should be used without care. Proper identification is important, and so is the understanding that the active ingredients in herbs can be taken in excess. The following recipe for mint tea is one that Valerie often recommends—both to her make-believe patients at King's Landing and to her modern-day friends. It's especially good for those suffering from headache or stomach distress.

Mint Tea

Cut sprigs of peppermint or spearmint fresh from the garden and rinse them quickly in cool water. Pack loosely into a china tea pot and cover with freshly boiled water. Steep for 15 to 20 minutes. Enjoy clear or with a bit of honey.

Darlene Love
Kingston

Retired schoolteacher Darlene Love suffers from fibromyalgia; this disease puts her in great pain, which she had great difficulty finding a way to successfully treat. In fact, nothing gave her real relief until she started gardening. But now that she's a devoted herb grower, she has been able to cope with the illness much better. She finds that the work and the satisfaction of gardening is a real distraction; when gardening, she forgets about her fibromyalgia. "Gardening has helped because it keeps my mind and body busy," she says. "It keeps me moving constantly, which has helped stop stiffness."

Working in one century and living in another makes herbalist Valerie Marr's life unique.

Darlene started her love affair with herbs in the mid 1990s by planting a few pots on her deck. It wasn't long before she moved on to a small planting bed near a cottage on the property, a quaint building in a hollow below the house, which once served as her husband's sugar shack for maple syrup production. After its renovation into a homey place with a kitchen and eating area, Darlene found its setting to be naturally private and just perfect for a garden. Her planting here is accented by her son's intricate and unusual sculptures, which hang from the cottage's outside walls for an appealing combination of garden and art.

There was really no initial design for the garden. As she worked at expanding a bed, she might come upon a boulder and have to move around it. When she ran out of space near the cottage, she started planting around the sides of a pond. Each time she decided to expand, her husband used a tractor to prepare the soil for her. She would then set things in place and see if she actually liked the way it was turning out. On one occasion, she spent a fair bit of time planting a large number of herb seedlings in a single, long row—only to realize that the final effect wasn't at all pleasing to her eye. Out they came, to be replanted in "little rooms" accented with a gravel mulch.

Darlene once worried she might be putting a plant in the wrong place, that something might spread too much if she didn't situate it correctly. "But now I don't care," she says. "I have plants reseeding themselves all over the garden, and I never worry about it." In fact, she considers a herb's tendency to readily reseed itself merely nature's way of helping her with her planting chores: she simply takes a flat of small pots with her to the garden each spring and, with a spoon, scoops little seedlings into them. These are then moved to her small greenhouse to grow until they find a home in the garden of a friend or neighbour; any excess plants go to the compost pile.

Gardening with herbs is mental and physical therapy for Darlene Love, who suffers from fibromyalgia.

Mint is a worry for most herb growers. But Darlene has learned to curtail this herb's tendency to take over an entire garden by planting it in 25 cm-long sections of open-ended fiberglass pipe, sunk directly into the ground. The length of pipe is buried deeply enough so that the mint's root systems are unable grow out from under it.

Darlene's favourite herb is rosemary because its fragrance is so invigorating. She uses it to make a hair rinse and adds it to potpourri, which she creates as a gift for friends. But rosemary can't be wintered outdoors in cold climates, so her next favourite species is thyme, fairly hardy in a New Brunswick garden. "There are so many different types of thyme, each with a slightly different fragrance."

Another favourite is verbascum, a strikingly handsome herb fashionable in English country gardens. Verbascum is a biennial species, which means it grows nothing but foliage the first summer, flowering only in its second year. Darlene's garden is home to dozens of varieties of verbascum started from seed ordered in Britain. Some varieties are miniatures that produce flower stalks less than one half metre in height; others are absolute giants, with stalks of flowers as tall as 2.5 metres. "I love the big rosette of leaves that they produce," says Darlene. "They have silvery leaves that are so soft to the touch, and that give off a subtle glow in the moonlight."

Gardening with herbs is mental and physical therapy for Darlene Love; in her world, herbs and wellness go hand in hand. Below is a recipe for rosemary hair rinse, one of Darlene's specialties. Using it after your shampoo is one of the quickest and easiest ways to improve hair shine.

Rosemary Hair Rinse

1 tbsp rosemary leaves
4 cups boiling water
1 tbsp cider vinegar

In a glass bowl, pour the boiling water over the rosemary leaves and let infuse until the liquid is cool. Strain well and add the vinegar. Pour over hair and massage into the scalp. Rinse with cool water.

The Secrets of Gardening with Herbs

- Grow herbs in a sunny location.
- Plant herbs where soil is well drained.
- Don't fertilize herbs excessively or they'll be less flavourful and fragrant.
- Don't set basil transplants out in the garden until soil is very warm.
- Keep flowers pinched from basil to encourage continued growth of leaves.
- Harvest herbs in mid-morning, after dew has dried from their leaves.
- Let potted rosemary plants dry out a little between waterings.
- Overwinter french tarragon indoors because, like rosemary, this is a tender herb.
- Cut chives just as they are beginning to form flowers, to encourage new shoot growth.
- Grow mint in open-ended lengths of recycled pipe (buried at least 25 cm in the ground) to contain its spreading nature.
- Use medicinal herbs at the advice of a knowledgeable practitioner.
- Let herbs go to seed so you'll have a ready source of new plants each spring (any excess can be composted).

A Selection of Herbs for New Brunswick Gardens

Herb	Plant Type	Growing Tips
anise hyssop	perennial	Seed directly in garden
basil	annual	Start 8 weeks early indoors
beebalm	perennial	Start with divisions
chamomile	annual	Seed directly in garden
chervil	annual	Seed directly in garden every 2 weeks
chives	perennial	Start with divisions or seed directly in garden
coriander	annual	Seed directly in garden every 2 weeks
dill	annual	Seed directly in garden; hates transplanting
feverfew	perennial	Seed directly in garden
lavender	perennial	Start with transplants; protect over winter
lemon balm	perennial	Seed directly in garden; keep clipped
lovage	perennial	Start with transplants
marjoram	annual	Seed directly in garden
mint	perennial	Start with transplants; restrict roots with collar
oregano	perennial	Seed directly in garden
parsley	perennial	Treat as an annual and seed directly each spring
rosemary	annual	Take indoors over winter
sage	perennial	Treat as an annual and seed directly each spring
summer savory	annual	Seed directly in garden
sweet cecily	perennial	Seed directly in garden
tarragon	annual	Start with transplants
thyme	perennial	Start with transplants

Generally speaking, herbs do best in the sunniest spot in the garden, in well-drained soil.

Herb Thoughts

*Oh! To have the thyme to smell sweet cecily,
to plumb the basil depths of parsley,
to know and love rosemary!
To make a lavender smell of wormwood, borage through the
feverfew and capture elecampane.
To hyssop the lovage of lemon balm and say in the
lemon verbena that the marjoram shall rule oregano!
We will mint our future or caraway our bodies to cilantro and
calm ourselves with chamomile in the corianders of fame, wrapped
in fennel—these places in the mind!*

—Ken Peck

How To Keep Deer Out Of The Garden

nless you live and garden in the middle of the city, it's possible that, at some point, you'll be forced to deal with the voracious appetite that white-tailed deer have for many types of garden vegetables, flowering plants, shrubs, and trees. Although graceful and placid-looking, these four-legged friends of the forest are not friends of the garden. Deer often leave the shelter of natural woodlands to voyage into residential backyards that border their usual habitat. They'll visit late in the evening or early in the morning, when things are quiet and peaceful. Corn, fruit, and leafy crops are their favourites, along with the tips of fruit trees and the tender foliage of hostas, daylilies, and chrysanthemums. Worst of all, deer are routine feeders, so once they target a certain garden or landscape (usually because it contains a collection of their most-loved munchies), it's difficult to discourage them from making successive visits!

Other than having a dog constantly patrolling the backyard, perhaps the best control strategy (and one of the most expensive lines of attack) is to construct a fence. Page-wire fences must be between eight and ten feet high to provide effective protection from deer. Another alternative that seems to work is to construct two three-foot-high fences made of three strings each, placing one fence behind the other, about three feet apart. This type of barrier seems to confuse deer because they are reluctant to jump over a fence if another one is visible just behind.

A fence of similar design—but one that uses electric shock as a deterrent—is called the New Hampshire Three-Wire Fence. It consists of an outer and an inner fence, the outer fence having strands of electrified wire set at heights of 15 and 36 inches. The inner fence, which is three feet inside the outer one, has a single strand of electrified wire set at a height of 27 inches. Experts swear by this system, but it's costly to install and can be hazardous for people as well as for deer.

Various types of repellents have been recommended for controlling the number of visits that deer make to a garden. Some are based on smell, others on taste. Raw egg sprays, strong-smelling soap, blood meal, urine, and human hair are odour-based repellents that have been used with varying degrees of success by gardeners and orchardists. Most of these substances must be applied at frequent intervals to protect crops from deer.

Hot pepper sauce, fresh or powdered garlic and onion, and various other types of untasty mixtures are also used to discourage deer. But any type of repellant that relies on a bad-taste experience also requires the deer to take at least a sample of a treated plant. This could result in a large amount of damage before deer realize just how unpleasant their garden snack really is. And, like odour-based deterrents, those based on taste must be applied on a routine basis. Generally speaking, deer aren't finicky eaters, but it has been shown that they usually dislike plants that have fuzzy leaves, spines, or a strong taste. The leaves of lamb's ears (*Stachys bysantina*) are covered with fine grey hairs, making them quite safe from deer. The thorns of barberry bushes (*Berberis thunbergii*) and the poisonous strong taste of monkshood (*Aconitum napellus*) are also plant features that have kept deer away. Other ornamental flowering plants have, for unknown reasons, been found to be less than tasteful to deer—including the plants listed below.

Gardeners who live close to natural deer habitats have a real challenge to face when deciding what to include in their plots. Growing deer-resistant plants may be the answer to an overnight garden pillage by local white-tails. Unfortunately, hungry deer have unpredictable pallets. It's not always a matter of taste!

Deer-Resistant Plants

Botanical Name	Common Name
Aquilegia sp.	columbine
Astilbe sp.	astilbe
Dicentra spectabilis	bleeding heart
Narcissus tazetta	daffodils
Digitalis purpurea	foxgloves
Iris sp.	iris
Helianthus annus	sunflowers
Delphinium formosum	delphiniums
Hesperus matronalis	dame's rocket
Paeonia officinalis	peonies
Rudbeckia hirta	rudbeckia
Geranium sp.	scented geraniums
Lobularia maritima	alyssum
Antirrhinum majus	snapdragons
Papaver sp.	poppies
Mentha sp.	mint
Lavendula officinalus	lavender
Thymus sp.	thyme
Achillea miffefolium	yarrow
Salvia officinalis	sage
Tanacetum vulgaris	tansy
Syringa vulgaris	lilacs
Forsythia intermedia	forsythia
Potentilla sp.	potentilla
Buddleia davidii	butterfly bush
Rosa rugosa	rugosa rose

Deer often leave the shelter of natural woodlands to voyage into residential backyards.

Hal Hinds, Fredericton

ROCK GARDENS

"My next-door neighbour, Mrs. Jones,
Has got a garden full of stones:
A crazy path, a lily pond,
A rockery, and, just beyond,
A sundial with a strange device,
Which Mrs. Jones thinks rather nice.

My next-door neighbour, Mrs. Jones,
Puts little plants between the stones.
They are so delicate and small
They don't mean anything at all.
I can't think how she gets them in,
Unless she plants them with a pin.

My next-door neighbour, Mrs. Jones,
Once asked me in to see her stones.
We stood and talked about a flower
For quite a quarter of an hour.
"Where is this lovely thing?" I cried.
"You're standing on it," she replied.

Reginald Arkell, 1934

In the 1700s, the noted explorer and natural historian Sir Joseph Banks constructed a rock garden at Chelsea, England, with a quantity of lava rock he had obtained in Iceland and a large amount of stone from the Tower of London. He probably didn't realize that he was starting a trend. Three centuries later, rock gardens—or "rockeries"—are found worldwide. Some are famous, like the one at the Royal Botanical Gardens at Kew, England. Others are not so famous and are found in simple backyard settings. All have rocks in them, of course, but some are elaborate replicas of a sloped, mountaintop environment where unique (and often tiny) alpine plants are grown, while others aren't much more than a jumble of stones with a few plants in between. Some take advantage of an existing rocky outcrop, while others are built around imported boulders and artificially-sculptured mounds of earth. One design isn't necessarily more authentic or pleasing to the eye than another; like any garden, it's all a matter of personal creation and choice. The following New Brunswickers are all rock gardeners, but their approaches to the task are remarkably different.

Erwin Landauer
Sisson Ridge

Just as it takes a sturdy breed of plants to withstand the growing conditions typical of mountainous regions, so it takes a patient and determined gardener to re-create such an environment in his or her own backyard. Picture a setting resembling a natural outcropping of rock on an exposed mountain in Turkey or Tibet. Imagine growing conditions characterized by gravelly, well-drained soil. Think about a sloped terrain exposed to the heat of the sun and to ravaging wind. Such are the requirements of alpine plants, and such is the description of the garden landscape of devoted alpine plant grower Erwin Landauer.

Back in 1953, when Erwin arrived in Canada from Austria, he didn't consider himself a gardener. But slowly, during the first years that he and his family lived in their home on Sisson Ridge near Plaster Rock, New Brunswick, he began to grow a vegetable garden and a variety of common bedding plants. About twenty years later, he built a small greenhouse to get an early start on his tomato plants. (After all, the growing season in his part of the province is quite short, so it's important to set out relatively mature plants after the last spring frost in order to guarantee a harvest before the first killing temperatures return in the fall.) But it wasn't until the late 1980s that Erwin actually became a plant collector. That's when he started to grow roses and peonies and lupins and clematis in earnest. He terraced the slope behind his home with cedar logs and started to garden with perennials. He built cold frames and a compost bin, and began to keep a detailed record of the number and variety of plants. Growing things became Erwin's favourite pastime, and he developed a preference for certain types of plants.

In the last five years, Erwin has become a keen alpine gardener. Today, the small plants found high in the mountains of faraway countries are his all-consuming interest, and he has transformed his landscape into an extraordinary rock garden that's home to an amazing variety of these alpine species—most of which he has grown from seed.

Erwin Landauer's rock garden is home to a variety of alpine species.

Erwin actually grows alpine plants all year round, with 48 feet of lighted bench space in his basement, where, each winter, he starts at least two hundred new types of alpines (and the occasional common perennial). He gets the seeds for these species from fellow members of both the Ontario and the North American Rock Garden Societies, as well as from seed catalogues and Internet sources. Some of these plants—such as a wonderful *Frittilaria forbassi* with grass-like leaves and charming little nodding flowers—take as long as five years to reach blooming size; others are so tiny, even at maturity, that they must be carefully marked when put in the garden so that they're not accidentally lost or trampled. Many seedlings are kept in pots in a cold frame for two or three years, until Erwin can determine whether or not they're sufficiently worthy of being planted permanently in his garden.

This fantastic rock garden, home to most of the one thousand species of plants in the Landauer collection, is built on a slope anchored by a wall of interlocking brick, and criss-crossed by a series of flagstone paths. The growing medium in this garden is a mixture of sand, peat-based potting mix, and topsoil. Stones and boulders are strategically placed, and crushed gravel is used as a mulch. According to Erwin, "a rock garden should be very free draining because alpine plants don't like soggy conditions." "And," he notes, "most of them need full sun, so it's important to plant them so they aren't completely in the shade of the stones or boulders around them."

His planting arrangement is pleasing to the eye. Rocks of different colours, shapes, and sizes have been placed at interesting angles and in attractive groupings. A creeping bellflower has been planted between crevices in the retaining wall, along with woolly thyme and perennial alyssum. Dozens of species of hens and chickens—some covered with soft grey hairs, others with hues of red or grey to their leaves—are interspersed with different species of sedum, dianthus, and blue gentian. Alpine primula (so tiny one almost needs a magnifying glass to notice them) are scattered throughout, and a large clump of rose daphne, with its wonderfully fragrant blooms, grows at the top of the slope. All plants have identification tags to go with them, even though Erwin is good at keeping their botanical names on the tip of his tongue. But he tucks these labels under the rock closest to the plant, rather than sticking them upright in the ground, so they don't detract from the natural look of the rockery. Plant names in the collection are also stored in Erwin's computer and, because he recently got a digital camera, many of his computer files are now electronically-illustrated with pictures of his own specimens.

Many summer days are spent monitoring the growth and development of each specimen, and he's constantly chasing weeds, which threaten to choke his precious alpines. "I have hundreds of acres of pasture land around this garden" he laments, "and all of it is a source for weed seeds to blow in from." He routinely adds new species or transplants things from one garden spot to another. There's never an end to what needs attention, but when he does take a break it's usually to just enjoy watching his alpine collection thrive in a place so remote from its normal habitat.

Wilma Allair
North Road, Campobello

"I'm gardening on a rock," says Wilma Allair, describing the restrictions of her garden on the north side of Campobello Island. "So that makes me a rock gardener, I suppose." In fact, her entire property has so little soil that she had to import some in order to be able to grow much of anything. She tells lots of tales about trying to find a place to put plants in the landscape—including her lilac adventure. "I wanted to put in two lilac bushes one year," she says, "but when I went around poking with a spade to try to locate a planting spot, I couldn't find a single place where I didn't hit bedrock just under the surface of the lawn." It was impossible. There just wasn't any place for lilacs here.

Wilma and her husband have lived at this scenic setting on Campobello for almost twenty years. Their house dates back to the 1850s, and is beautifully placed at the base of a rocky ledge, with a stretch of open lawn behind, extending to the sea's edge. The entire property is on a rocky outcrop that juts into the waters of Head Harbour Passage, with an uninterrupted line of sight across the channel to Eastport, Maine. Wilma often looks at the mainland with envy, thinking about the topsoil that gardeners over there have to work with. But she turns her attention back to her island garden, which she has transformed into a

Gardening along rocky shores is a challenge for Wilma Allair of Campobello Island.

marvellous place, rocks and all. "It's been the hardest garden I've ever done, anywhere," she admits.

This gardener grew up in Medicine Hat, Alberta, just across the road from a commercial greenhouse. "As soon as I was big enough to carry a fifty-pound hose, they let me go to work there," she recalls, and it was a love affair thereafter. "I loved the chrysanthemums and the roses and the cut flowers," she says. Since that first horticultural experience, she has always enjoyed gardening and working with plants, wherever she's lived.

In her current garden, Wilma mixes various types of plants into her landscaping plan. She has a small raised-bed vegetable garden, a raspberry patch, a strawberry bed, and a herb collection grown in a cold frame to protect it from the chill of island nights. Pots of annuals are displayed with flair on the porch and walkway beside the house. And each year she fills planter pots to sit in nooks and crannies throughout her rock garden. She plants delightful combinations of bedding plants—red geraniums, purple wave and yellow flowered petunias, osteospermum, licorice plant—in the hanging baskets and window boxes that decorate her potting shed. Most of these annuals are grown in the small greenhouse, started every year in March. The greenhouse was originally intended to let her grow enough for her own needs, but because she's become quite well known for her successful seed sowing, she often ends up supplying many of her fellow island gardeners with overflow from her own efforts.

It's the rock garden, though, that really stands out on the Allair property. In the beginning, Wilma filled natural depressions in the ledge behind the house with soil brought from other parts of the island. To this, she added compost from her own pile, and well-aged manure brought home in the car in buckets from an off-island farm. Accumulating enough manure for her needs took several trips, she recalls, all of which were stinky adventures!

When Wilma had covered the rock ledge with the soil, manure, and compost, she began to plant, putting in common rockery plants like sedum, ground phlox, hens and chickens, artemesia, and stonecrops. Colourful annuals were added, such as bunny tail ornamental grass, salvia, dusty miller, celosia, snap dragons, and cheery clumps of nasturtium. She placed these annuals among marine artifacts—for example, a huge steel boat anchor—and among pieces of driftwood collected from the shore. It's a perfect combination for a seaside garden.

In areas where there was a slightly deeper pocket of soil in the rocks, Wilma decided to try some of her favourite perennials. She planted cranesbill, lilies, yarrow, astilbe, hosta, and sundrops (which she calls "Missouri primroses") along with spreading junipers and ferns. She has had poor luck, over the years, with some of these perennial plants—mostly due to problems overwintering in such a windswept location, and to too little moisture in the heat of summer. In recent years, to help her rock garden cope with extended periods of drought, she has installed a soaker hose watering system by snaking a perforated rubber tube through various levels of the ledge. When rain doesn't fall often enough, she can turn it on and have fresh water reach plants in all of the rock's crevices.

Gardening along the rocky shores of an island is, at best, a challenge. Shallow soil, lack of moisture, and on-shore breezes are an unavoidable part of the landscape. But, as the saying goes, "when you've been given lemons, make lemonade." Wilma Allair's garden is an example of making the very best from the conditions of your particular landscape. Given rock, she made a rock garden!

Hal Hinds
Fredericton

When you've exposed yourself to the world of nature and the life of plants as long as Hal Hinds, you might have a tendency to look at gardening a bit differently. Without question, Hal enjoys the usual pleasure that gardeners get from working with the soil, from watching seeds germinate and mature into healthy specimens, from growing one's own food, and from getting lots of exercise while creating a landscape. But because he's a trained botanist and ecologist, and because his career has focussed on teaching university students about plant science and taxonomy, he often thinks of his garden as a place to re-create natural ecosystems, rather than as a space to manicure and manipulate into flower beds.

Being an expert on New Brunswick's native plants, Hal uses his garden as a place to safeguard some of the province's most unique species. Being interested in the way plants grow in suitable environments, he has often tried his hand at re-creating bits of mother nature, right in the middle of a city. And always a lover of art and beauty, he keeps sections of his garden for brightly-coloured flowers, twining vines, and statuesque shrubs and trees. In this way, Hal's garden is an extension of himself.

He moved to his current Fredericton home about fifteen years ago. At that time, it was a derelict site with a house in a terrible state of repair. There was a long, narrow piece of land that sloped to the northeast, with no horticultural planting. The soil was heavy clay with lots of natural springs, surrounded by mature shade trees on neighbouring lots. It was a garden-in-waiting, and Hal was a gardener-with-a-mission.

At that point, Hal had already been gardening for a long time, most often with wildflowers and native species. He'd worked at "The Garden In The Woods," a private botanic garden in Framingham, Massachusetts, where he was involved with collecting seeds and seedlings of local wildflowers to use in creating naturalistic gardens. He had also been a part-time organic farmer, aiming for food self-sufficiency while practising environmentally-sustainable agriculture.

Before he started working on his present garden, Hal had developed another interest: a passion for primroses and an admiration for alpine plants. "I love the great diversity of the genus *Primula*," he enthuses. "There are primulas on almost all continents, and there is a tremendous variation in their shapes, sizes, flower colours, and preferred habitats." He finds "all alpine plants interesting in their own way." The challenge of growing them, he admits, "is to maintain a balance between the size of the plants and the rocky terrain in which they are placed."

This size and scale of a mountaintop is something Hal knows intimately from collecting plants and seeds in alpine or subalpine sites in much of eastern Canada, during botanical research field trips. Through seed exchanges with friends and relatives, and with various rock garden clubs, he received mountainous plant material from all over the world.

When Hal finally decided to mould part of his garden into a habitat that had a place for both of his favourite species, he had to consider certain design requirements. He knew that he wanted to express his love of the mountains and the neat, bright flowering plants that are found there by creating a rocky oasis in his backyard. And he also wanted to create the moisture-loving conditions preferred by his favourite primulas, the Auriculars. He wanted it to seem as if the alpines were actually growing on a mountain side, and as if the primulas were in an equally naturalistic setting.

"There were two large boulders towards the back of the property, which I used to begin the rock garden plantings. Later I created several other rocky mounds, which I planted with alpine saxifrages, alpine primulas, corydalis, violets, aquilegia, hens and chickens, sedum, and other small rock garden plant subjects." He had great success with some of these plants and lots of trials with others. "It's sometimes difficult to keep alpines thriving at our lower altitude, with its less intense sun, its often soggy and hot summers, and our long and cold winters." But each alpine he plants is one to pamper and cosset, just to see how it will do in this re-created terrain.

In addition to his mountain garden, Hal needed more rocks for his next project. He created a pond into which he channelled many of the springs that dapple the property, augmenting the heavy clay soil with great quantities of organic matter and sand, and placing rocks and stepping stones to make the whole thing look like a small lake. The results were pleasing but they were also, much to his delight, the makings of a perfect habitat for primulas. He started with several common European cowslips (*Primula veris*), which grew so vigorously that, within a few growing seasons, they seeded themselves over the rest of the garden. The two horticultural varieties of *Primula* x *pruhoniciana* that he had been given by friend and fellow botanist Mary Young grew equally magnificently. From these first primulas he went on to grow many others, and now has "nearly 75 different species and cultivars." One of his secrets to success, he feels, is that he "often mulches with small, crushed rock to reflect the heat and hold in the moisture"; primulas never like to dry out.

Hal's successful cultivation of his rock garden plants and his much-loved primroses came from tending to their growth requirements by mimicking their natural environment—a life's botanical study and a simple love of plants, all in one garden.

The Secrets of Rock Gardens

- Create a rock garden to grow typical rock garden plants, or to make a garden out of a rocky spot in your landscape.
- Choose a place that receives abundant sunshine, because rock garden plants prefer lots of light.
- Select rocks of different sizes, shapes, and colours to show the plants off to their best advantage.
- Add lots of organic matter to the soil, and, if necessary, work in coarse sand to improve drainage.
- Consider mulching around your rock garden plants with gravel, in order to retain moisture and an even soil temperature.
- Water your rock garden plants during extended dry spells.

Suitable Plants for New Brunswick Rock Gardens

- *Arctostaphylos uva-ursi* (bearberry) - a spreading evergreen with glossy leaves and small, whitish-pink flowers followed by red fruit.
- *Alyssum saxatile* (basket of gold) - a sprawling herbaceous perennial with grey leaves and masses of yellow blossoms in the spring.
- *Cotoneaster horizontalis* (rock-spray cotoneaster) - a shrub that spreads in a horizontal fashion with small, shiny leaves and red berries in the fall.
- *Daphne cneorum* (rose daphne) - a sprawling evergreen with small clusters of sweet-smelling pink flowers.
- *Juniperus horizontalis* (creeping juniper) - a spreading evergreen with soft, blue-green needles.
- *Achillea* sp. (yarrow) - a herbaceous perennial with grey, feathery foliage and white, pink, or yellow flowers, depending on the species.
- *Aquilegia canadensis* (wild columbine) - a herbaceous perennial with tiny red flowers.
- *Arabis caucasica* (rock cress) - a herbaceous perennial with mats of pure white flowers in early spring.
- *Campanula* sp. (bellflower) - a vigorous, herbaceous perennial with blue, bell-like flowers.
- *Corydalis* sp. (corydalis) - a dainty herbaceous perennial related to bleeding heart.
- *Gentiana* sp. (gentian) - a low growing herbaceous perennial with deep blue blossoms.
- *Iberis sempervirens* (candytuft) - a striking herbaceous perennial with masses of white flowers in early spring.
- *Saponaria ocymoides* (soapwort) - a trailing herbaceous perennial for draping over rocks.
- *Sedum acre* (goldmoss stonecrop) - a crawling herbaceous perennial with bright yellow flowers.
- *Sedum spectabile* (autumn joy) - a taller sedum (grows up to 18 inches or 45 cm) with blood red flowers in the fall.
- *Sempervivens* sp. (hens and chickens) - a fleshy herbaceous perennial that forms clusters of daughter plantlets around the parent.
- *Thymus serpyllum* (mother of thyme) - a creeping herbaceous perennial with dainty pink flowers.
- *Viola tricolour* (Johnny jump-ups) - an annual that seeds itself readily and has pansy-like flowers.

John and Lola Miller, Bathurst

WATER GARDENS

"I have left almost to the last the magic of water, an element which owing to its changefulness of form and mood and colour and to the vast range of its effects is ever the principal source of landscape, beauty, and has like music a mysterious influence over the mind."

Sir George Sitwell, 1909

There's just something about water in a landscape. It can gently trickle over a jumble of interesting stones and collect in a quiet, reflective pool, or it can cascade over impressive ledges into an elaborately-designed concrete pond. It might be found in a formal setting with spouting fountains and ornate stone sculpture, or in an intimate, secret corner at the back of the garden. A water garden can be as elaborate as pumps and liners and filters will allow, but as simple as a large ceramic or wooden container with a water lily floating in it. Wherever there is water there is added sight and sound, and an opportunity to grow plants that aren't happy in any other setting.

I've always intended to have a water garden near the deck at the back of the house, because that's where we spend lots of time in the summer; it's where I thought I'd be able to most enjoy the calming sound of water gurgling in the quiet of the evening. But because I usually have so many other garden chores to look after each spring—getting perennial beds weeded and vegetable seeds sown—it was always a project that landed on the "to-do list."

However, when I was offered a waterproof fibreglass tank, about a metre square and 25 cm deep, I thought I could get a start on the project. I intended to set the tank into the ground and create at least the impression of a small pond, disguising its edges with rocks and adding some interesting shells and stones from family rambles at the seashore.

Although it wouldn't have a pump to circulate water and create that lovely sound, it would at least give me a place to grow water hyacinth, water lettuce, some marsh marigolds, and a bit of duck weed—all plants that like to either float in water or grow in water-saturated soil. And I've never had those conditions in my garden.

I soon realized the futile nature of the entire plan. I'd filled the tank with water, just to have a place for a water hyacinth I'd been given by a friend, while I got the rest of the installation completed. Within hours, our dog had found what he considered to be a ready-made swimming hole, complete with floating play toys just for his use. I found him sloshing around in the tank and the water hyacinth in pieces, all over the lawn. So much for my idea of a water garden.

But the people whose gardens are featured in this chapter have had much more success with their attempts to have the enjoyment of water in their landscapes. Not one of them has a golden retriever!

GAIL TAYLOR
COVERED BRIDGE GARDENS, ST. GEORGE

Gail Taylor was in the process of creating a display garden for her nursery business when she decided that she wanted a water garden. She was intending to provide customers with ideas for using some of the herbaceous perennials, ornamental grasses,

Gail Taylor grows her water lilies in pots, which she places in the deepest part of the pond. By having them in containers, lilies can easily be lifted out in the fall.

ferns, and shrubs she sold from her "Covered Bridge Gardens" near St. George. And a water garden seemed perfect for a sunny spot in the middle of her lawn, between her home and her commercial-sized greenhouse.

Gail and her husband Stephen began digging in the fall of 1993. But they knew that rocks would come to the surface in the hole when next spring's frost left the ground, so they waited until the beginning of the next growing season to finish the work. "It's important to get all of the rocks removed from the walls and bottom of any proposed pond area," explains Gail, "so they don't work their way through over time and make a hole in the liner."

At the end of the winter, Gail and Stephen removed the protruding rocks and covered the base of the hole with a 4 cm layer of fine sand to act as a buffer between the ground and the pond liner. On top of the sand went a thick layer of moist newspaper, for a bit of added liner protection. Finally, a 3.5 m by 4 m section of 40 ml "pvc" rubber liner material was draped over the hole. As the bottom of the pond was slightly cone shaped, Gail had to taper and fold the liner.

"In the middle, the pond is 43 centimetres deep," describes Gail, "but we made a ledge, all around the inside walls, that's only 15 centimetres down." Water lilies (*Nyphaea* sp.) grow well in pots placed in the deepest part of the pond. By having them in containers, the lilies can be easily lifted out in the fall for overwintering indoors (they won't survive when the pond freezes each December). Water lilies grow from rhizomes, which can be purchased at garden centres each spring. Before adding rhizomes to a pond, plant them horizontally in clay-rich, mucky soil in plastic mesh baskets, or in ordinary plant pots that have good drainage holes. And if the pond has fish, it's always a good idea to put a layer of coarse sand or pea gravel on top of the pot's soil surface to keep rhizomes from being eaten by hungry swimmers!

Gail also places pots of Japanese iris and sweet flag in her pond, but these plants prefer a shallower depth, so she sets them on the ledge. Japanese iris (*Iris kaempferi*) have long, grass-like leaves that will grow to heights of 54 cm. The plant's roots can be completely submerged in the summer, but do best at shallow depths of between 4 cm and 20 cm. There are iris varieties with blossoms of white, pink, violet, and blue, flowering in early to mid-summer.

Sweet flag (*Acorus calamus*) is one of New Brunswick's native wetland plants. Its leaves are similar to those of the Japanese iris but are wider at the base and of a lighter green; some varieties even have green-and-cream-striped variegated leaves. All these plants give off a sweet fragrance when their foliage is bruised or crushed, and grow well when roots are submerged in shallow water. In midsummer, sweet flag produce small, brownish-green flowers that look a bit like a cat-tail.

To complete the installation, Gail surrounded the edge of her pond with a collection of flagstones and beach rocks. "I wanted to make it look natural," she admits, "so I took a fair bit of time to place the stones." She matched edges and shapes, and made sure that the liner's top was obscured from view. Floating plants completed the picture. For example, she added water hyacinth (*Eichhornia crassipes*), which has clusters of heart-shaped, glossy green leaves with thick, air-filled stalks that help keep the plant at the water's surface; water hyacinth produce showy blue flowers in the middle of the summer.

Gail also added free-floating water lettuce (*Pistia stratiotes*), which has a rosette of leaves than fan out from the base of the plant—much like those of romaine lettuce. Over the summer, water lettuce will form daughter plants on runner-like offshoots, and grow long feathery roots that trail in the water. Unfortunately, both water lettuce and water hyacinth are tender plants that won't survive a New Brunswick winter; however, they can easily be brought inside in the fall and kept growing in a lighted aquarium until the next season, when they can be returned to their outdoor water garden.

Many water gardens have some sort of filter and circulation system to keep water clear and clean. "I didn't put a pump in this pond," says Gail, "because it's too far away from an electrical outlet." She finds that the water gets a bit of a greenish tinge, from an excess of algae, only in midsummer, after a long period with little rain. She knows that her pond plants are pumping oxygen into the water, because the goldfish she added are always healthy.

And she does top up the water level if there isn't enough rain to do the job. "I also clean the pond out every spring," she says, to keep debris from collecting in the bottom. She does this by siphoning the pond's water out into a barrel, washing the liner with a hose, scooping out the leaves and dirty water that collect in the pond bottom during the washing process, and, finally, by replacing the water that she took out in the first place. "I find all sorts of treasures when I'm cleaning the bottom of the pond"—including snails, water bugs, and worms.

After the water is replenished, Gail returns the plants (overwintered indoors) to their proper places. Within a short period of time, the frogs return to join them. "We've had frogs in the pond an hour after we filled it for the first time," Gail confides, "and they've been there every year since." She enjoys watching them sit on the stones at the pond's edge and resting among the foliage of a surrounding perennial bed. These plants—daylilies, variegated grasses, sedum, woolly thyme, and hosta—make the setting appear lush and vibrant all summer long.

Now that her first pond is a well-established garden feature, Gail is at work on a bigger and better one behind the house. An ongoing project over the last few summers, it will be several times the size of her first pond, surrounded by more gardens full of her favourite foliage plants, such as hosta and variegated grasses. "I'll have some flowering plants too," she admits, "but I'm really interested in unusual combinations of leaf types these days." The new pond will be edged with granite boulders collected over the years at nearby quarries, and a waterfall will cascade over a series of flagstone ledges, supported by a pump pushing 160 gallons per minute. Gail intends to put the pump in a tub (sunk at the bottom of the pond) to keep it from being clogged with leaves and other debris. "It's a very good way to keep it clean and working at peak performance." She also suggests that anyone starting a water garden invest in the very best of liner material, because it's easier to build once, and be done with it, than it is to take things apart after a pond springs a leak!

Rod Lutes
Alma

Rod Lutes is an accomplished horticulturist who has taken on many botanical challenges during his career, including management of the award-winning golf course at Fundy National Park. So when he was deciding on something new to add to his garden, outside a lovely old home in Alma, he was looking for something different—something that involved unusual design and installation strategies. The idea of a water feature was appealing. It was the spring of 1998, and he'd helped a friend install a pond the previous year, which had given him a bit of incentive to put in his own. "But I decided to start from scratch, rather than with a pre-designed kit," he says, because he was planning to install it between two existing perennial beds in a sunny spot near the centre of the backyard.

The pond area ended up being approximately 2 metres by 3 metres in size, with an overall water depth of 60 cm. "I wanted to put two shelves along the sides," says Rod, "so that I could grow marginal plants." One shelf was created at the front of the pond, at a depth of 20 cm, with the other closer to the back, 30 cm below the water surface. "These shelves had to be taken into consideration when calculating the liner size," he says, which is an important part of the process of pond construction. "It's better to get a big-enough piece of liner to begin with," says Rod, "rather than trying to patch things together after you find that you haven't got sufficient material to cover the entire hole." Rod used heavy-duty polyethylene and bought enough to cover the bottom, the sides, and the edges so that it could be held in place with stones. Before putting the liner in place, he added a thick section of floor carpeting to the bottom of the hole to keep rocks from piercing through.

After filling the pond with water, Rod installed a small pump to spill water over a collection of stones. "It gives me that water-trickle sound," he explains, "and it adds oxygen to the water." He finds that he has to top the water level up about once a month, but because he gets his supply from a well, he can add it directly to the pond. "People on a municipal supply should be worried about chlorine affecting their pond's fish," cautions Rod. Chlorinated tap water should be left in large buckets to sit for a few days so that chlorine will evaporate, leaving the water appropriate for any type of water garden wildlife.

During the first summer, Rod kept ordinary goldfish in his water garden. "They were no problem at all, and they helped to keep the mosquito population down." He'd only put in six fish at the beginning of the season, but by fall, when it came time to prepare the pond for the winter, he took out well over two hun-

One summer, Rod Lutes put six ordinary goldfish into his water garden; by fall, there were over two hundred fish.

dred! "Most of these I gave away to anyone who would take then, and the rest I carted to a pet shop which gladly took them off my hands." The next summer Rod switched to fantail goldfish, which he found had far less tendency to breed so profusely. "I only had two dozen extra fish at the end," he recounts with a sigh of relief.

Because his pond is relatively shallow, it freezes right to the bottom during the winter, so he always brings the fish indoors after several days of hard frost, and keeps them in an aquarium. He also brings in his water lilies, his calla lilies (*Zantedeschia ethiopica*) and his taro (*Colocasia esculenta*). "I pull the pots of water lilies out of the pond and leave them to drain for a day," he describes. "Then I cut their stems back to pot level and put the pruned plants into heavy plastic bags." After that they go into a cold room in his basement, where it's cool and dark. In late May, after all danger of frost is past, they're returned to the pond for another growing season. Pots of calla and taro are also brought indoors, and treated just like the rest of his houseplants all winter. "They can be allowed to dry out and go dormant," he suggests; in that case, the plants would be stored in a cool, dry spot over the winter, then repotted in the spring just before being set back in the pond.

Rod's water garden has given him so much enjoyment that he's considering making a new one in the near future. "I'm thinking of putting in another one so I can grow more varieties of water lilies…." Are these words from another addicted gardener?

John and Lola Miller
Bathurst

On a half-acre city lot in a quiet Bathurst neighbourhood, John and Lola Miller have taken to gardening in a big way. Over twenty years, this couple created a marvellous landscape that includes the private, foliage-rich appeal of a south-seas setting, the colourful blooms of a tropical paradise, a well-manicured collection of trees, vines, and perennials, a productive vegetable garden, a number of rock-rimmed terraces, and a secret garden room.

But it's their water garden that's perhaps the most entrancing feature of the whole property. Visible from the deck and framed by lush foliage, cheery flowering plants, and an attractive stone path, the large open pond and accompanying waterfall is an outstanding component of the landscape.

The Miller's water garden was begun a few years ago, with the digging of the base pond. The depression in the ground was formed into an oval shape, approximately four and a half metres in diameter at its widest point and tailored toward one end, where the waterfall would enter. The deepest part of the pond was in the centre, but John molded the sides to make a shelf at a depth of 30 cm around much of the circumference.

When earth removal was finished, John laid a heavy-duty liner over the bottom and sides of the hole, bringing the liner up to the lip of the pond, where he smoothed it over the soil in a shallow depression dug around the pond's edge. He then laid down a series of bricks, side by side, over the top of the liner, all around the pond. The liner was then drawn back toward the pond's centre, over this rim of bricks, so that a final edging of flagstones could be placed on top. These uppermost stones extended out over the pond's interior by 5 cm, creating an overhang to camouflage the top edge of the liner from view, and to make a shady place for the pond's fish.

Each piece of this flagstone fits against its neighbour like a glove, giving the pond's border a professional finish. "We rented a rock-cutting machine to help do the work," remembers John, "but it was still a long and tedious job." They only managed to cut and place five flagstones each evening, largely because of the time to make each cut, but also because the work created so much dust, says Lola, that they had to stop early enough to be able to hose down surrounding trees and flower beds before dark. "What a mess!"

With the pond built, they added plants. The couple had purchased bare-root water lily rhizomes from a local nursery and been told to pot them up in regular garden soil. "We had a hard time finding some that didn't have peat added to it," says Lola, but they managed to gather enough to plant two lilies per container. They inserted tablets of slow-release fertilizer at the base of each pot, and covered the soil surface with gravel. But because the entire planting process left the pots and the lilies covered with lots of dirt, they decided to clean them in a large garbage bucket filled with water. "This helped to rinse all of the fines from the soil in the pots and get the dirt away from the outside surface." It also meant there wasn't a cloud of mud released into the pond when the lilies were sunk to the bottom. The water lilies have remained in the pond every winter since they were first put in place. "We bought a special tool to allow us to reach far enough down in the water to insert the slow release fertilizer tablets in their pots each year," says Lola, but other than that the plants have been relatively maintenance free.

Visible from the deck and framed by lush foliage, John and Lola Miller's open pond is an outstanding component of their landscape.

On the pond's submerged shelf, Lola and John placed pots of marsh marigold, Japanese iris, arrow head (*Sagitarria sagittifolia*), blue flag iris (*Iris versicolor*), and dwarf papyrus (*Cyperus isocladus*). All but the dwarf papyrus are plants that are hardy through New Brunswick winters, so the Millers have been leaving them in the pond all year, with great success; dwarf papyrus is a more tender species, so they bring it indoors each fall. Variegated-leafed sweet flag (*Acorus calamus variegatus*) was planted in pots in the pond, but it overwinters best if removed from the water late in the season and planted directly in the ground.

"And each summer we purchase some water lettuce and some water hyacinth from a garden centre," adds Lola. "We usually start with just two or three plants of each variety, because they spread very quickly." She doesn't find it worthwhile to try to overwinter them indoors, as she'd rather use the space for other planting projects.

After the pond had been in place for two full summers, John began the work of creating a waterfall. This was almost as complicated as installing the water garden, because he wanted to make a tower of stones on two different levels, using large basalt boulders to create a mountainous effect. His son helped him get the stones from a nearby quarry, but the two men ended up making three trips to the site before enough rock was acquired—rock of an attractive black colour shot through with seams of the green mineral epidote. "There are approximately a hundred boulders in the falls," says John, "and they each weigh over two hundred kilos."

Using a heavy-duty dolly, John rolled each rock into the back of a rental truck, and then, when he got back to the house, down to the pond area of the garden. There, he made large holes in each one, using a rented drill with a special rock bit attached. The rocks were then moved into place and connected with huge bolts, each piece of the waterfall fitting together like a giant jigsaw puzzle.

Because the waterfall's peak is almost two metres above the pond's surface, John had to roll the topmost boulders up planks and slide them onto their bolts. In the centre of the structure he molded a bit of a depression, so that water would collect in a pool before completing its fall into the pond.

Circulating water around the pond and up over the falls is done with the help of two pumps, designed to push eight hundred gallons of water per hour. One of the pumps is at the base of the pond, resting on a brick to keep it away from dirt that could collect beneath it. This machine moves water from the bottom of the pond to the top to keep it full of oxygen for the fish and to filter it to keep the pond clear. The other pump is right at the base of the falls, connected to a piece of tubing that John attached to the top of the mound of basalt, so that it can move waters over the falls on a continuous basis.

Getting a source of electricity to the pumps was an ambitious enterprise. "I had to dig an eighteen-metre-long trench from the pond to the house to bury a special electrical cord," recounts John. "And then we had to have an electrician install the proper outlet for these to be plugged into before we could get properly hooked up."

With pond, waterfall, pumps, and plants in place, it was time for the Millers to add some fish. "We started with just a few goldfish, but have never had problems with them multiplying excessively," says Lola. She believes that population numbers level out according to how much space is available for growth. And she's had lots of success overwintering fish, mostly because the water in the centre of the pond is deep enough not to freeze solid. John did try to put a heater in place for the winter—the type usually used to keep cattle troughs open in cold spells—but he found that it was powerful enough to keep the entire pond open, which wasn't very healthy for either the plants around the rim, or for his power bill. So the Millers will be experimenting with that a bit more in upcoming winters, until they get a procedure that works best for them and for the living creatures in the water.

At the end of every August, John spreads a net over the surface of the pond to collect all of the leaves that fall from surrounding trees. "We don't want them falling into the water," he says, "because it has been shown that decomposing leaves leach toxins into the water that can kill fish if the concentration gets excessive." After all of the leaves are off the trees, he moves the net so that there's no chance it can sink into the water and get frozen in place. Other than that, and a bit of cleaning in the deepest part of the pond every other year, he doesn't anticipate much maintenance to keep the water garden looking its best.

As they continue to enjoy their pond and waterfalls, John and Lola will experiment with the plants that are part of this setting. Along with the submerged species, they've always had lovely assemblages of their regular garden favourites—around the outer rim of the pond plants like canna, new guinea impatiens, datura, hosta, and cut-leaf stephandra—but they're never opposed to trying something new. "We'd love to grow some different water lilies," Lola suggests, "and I'm always watching at nurseries and in mail-order catalogues for some new water garden species." That's the talk any gardener can relate to!

The Secrets of Water Gardens

- Pick a sunny location for your water garden because most plants that grow well in wet environments do best with lots of light.
- Consider purchasing a water garden kit if you're just getting started; these come complete with a pre-fabricated tank, circulating pump, and filter.
- Keep in mind that rocks might project from the hole you dig, so make sure to protect the liner material with a layer of sand or some old floor carpeting.
- Create different depths in your pond by making shelves around its rim, as some plants like to be submerged deeper than others.
- Overwinter tender pond plants indoors. Most hardy species can be kept right in the pond, especially if the water doesn't freeze all the way to the bottom.
- Top up the pond's water level with unchlorinated water, especially if you are keeping fish.
- Keep the water garden's pump elevated on a brick or set in a bucket at the bottom of the pond, so it doesn't get clogged with dirt and debris.

Harbour Park, St. Martins

Public Gardens

"The love of gardening is a seed that once sown never dies."

Gertrude Jekyll

It's hard to love gardening the way I do without wanting to spend as much time in gardens as possible. So if I'm not in my own, you'll probably find me in someone else's. Since becoming a gardening addict, I've spent a great amount of time visiting other gardens and gardeners. In the process I've been told many gardening stories, and been given many hints and suggestions to treasure and share.

However, during my visits to home gardens in places all across New Brunswick, I came to realize that the province has many public gardens designed and built by interesting people in unusual ways. Each one of these gardens is looked after by a gardener or group of gardeners, be they volunteers or paid employees, who get as much pleasure from their work as I get from my hobby. Some of these gardens have been community projects, while others are commercial or government ventures. Some have been built in memory of important people, and others are simply a beautiful addition to a park or public place. But all of these gardens are meant to give visitors pleasure—to the eye, to the nose, and to the spirit—and shouldn't be missed the next time you have a chance to leave your own garden for awhile.

Kingsbrae Horticultural Garden
St. Andrews

The Kingsbrae Horticultural Garden encompasses a 27-acre site overlooking the Passamaquoddy Bay in the seaside town of St. Andrews. In the few short years since its construction, the garden has blossomed into one of the region's most popular tourist destinations.

Kingsbrae has many integrated garden components to appeal to visitors. A "Cottage Garden" is enclosed by a painted stone wall near the entrance to the Visitor's Centre. This informal mixed border is home to annuals and perennials, fruit trees and climbers, all interplanted to ensure that something will always be in bloom.

Just outside of the Visitors Centre is the "Knot Garden," where smartly clipped boxwood, frilly groupings of rue, mounds of artemesia, clusters of lavender, and clumps of santolina have been intricately mixed to create the illusion of ropes of foliage fixed into lines and corners. This elaborate knot looks down on the "Rose Garden" where a collection of hardy, perennial rose bushes surround a variety of tender, hybrid Teas.

Gardeners fond of perennials will be impressed by Kingsbrae's centre showcase. Completely enclosed by a mature cedar hedge, and featuring raised beds radiating from a sundial placed in honour of Princess Diana, the "Perennial Garden" is home to both familiar and unusual varieties. Visitors to this section of Kingsbrae should plan to linger a bit to enjoy strains of classical music and the regular "knock" of a quaint Japanese water-torture fountain.

Canadian fruit tree heritage is being preserved in the Kingsbrae "Orchard," home to the estate's original apple trees, as well as younger trees of varieties like Sandow, New Brunswicker, Golden Russet, and Red Astrachan. At their feet is

Poa supina, a no-mow grass often used in the orchards and pastures of our ancestors. Below the orchard is a planting idea with true New Brunswick flair: a fiddlehead, formed from raised mounds of earth planted with thyme and blueberry bushes.

Then there's the rill (a slate-lined water course), the wildflower meadow, a working windmill, a bird and butterfly garden, the rockery, a heath and heather garden, a vegetable garden, a typical Charlotte-county vegetable garden, and a compost display. Visitors can also stroll along the Kingsbrae nature trail, which has interpretive signs describing the region's forest species. And time should be spared to visit the "Therapy Garden," created for those with special needs, or the "Children's Garden," which has plants to smell and feel, and a doll house just waiting for young adventurers.

But an absolutely memorable part of the Kingsbrae experience comes from a visit to its "White Garden," patterned after the famous white garden created by the poetical and romantic Vita Sackville-West and her husband Harold Nicolson at Sissinghurst Castle in Kent, England, and is an intriguing collection of plants—all with foliage and flowers that fit in the white spectrum of light. There's something about the colour white—with its related hues of silver and grey—that bring a sense of space, coolness, and serenity to a garden. That's why the horticulturists and landscape designers at Kingsbrae chose to focus on a white theme for one garden component at the garden's entrance. Their aim, according to garden manager Andreas Haun, is to provide a calming, soothing approach to the other sections of the garden. "The white garden sets the mood for the relaxing adventure that is a visit to Kingsbrae," adds Haun. "It slows people down and helps them prepare to enjoy an afternoon in the garden."

Like other types of gardens, a white garden needs a combination of plants that provide a display of blooms throughout the growing season. Kingsbrae has selected a variety of annuals,

Home to annuals, perennials, fruit trees, and climbers, this "Cottage Garden" is part of the 27-acre Kingsbrae Horticultural Garden.

perennials, shrubs, and trees that all have flowers or foliage in complementary colours of white, silver, and grey. "We mix and match everything," says Haun.

The front of the white garden is sculptured against a margin of turf and a brick-lined path, with its back against a cedar hedge and a variety of mature hardwoods. Tall perennials and shrubs have been placed at the rear of the border, while species with more compact growth thrive at the front.

Kingsbrae's white garden called for careful soil preparation prior to planting. Cover crops of buckwheat followed by winter rye were planted the season before the garden was actually created, in order to choke out weeds and to add nutrients and organic matter when these cover crops were tilled back into the soil.

Maintenance of the white garden begins with seeing that plants are properly nourished all summer. Kingsbrae horticulturists have had great success with an organic fertilizer that's made in New Brunswick from fish waste; it's used as a foliar spray. Compost, scratched into the soil surface, is also beneficial. When granular fertilizers are used, they're sprinkled over the bed's surface, then watered into the soil.

Spent flower blossoms are regularly removed from plants in the white garden to encourage repeat blooming. Tall or sprawling plants are staked (or otherwise supported) to keep them looking and growing their best. And an automatic water system provides a good soaking early in the morning, during the driest weeks of the summer. For gardeners keen on creating a white garden of their own, here are a number of good species to select:

SUGGESTIONS FOR WHITE GARDEN PERENNIALS FROM KINGSBRAE GARDEN (ZONE 4B - 5)

Botanical Name	Cultivar Name
Anenome x *hybrida*	Honorine Jobert
Artemesia absinthium	Lambrook Silver
Artemesia x	Powis Castle
Artemesia ludoviciana	Silver King
Astilbe x *arendsii*	Snowdrift
Boltonia asteroides	Snowbank
Campanula sp.	
Chrysanthemum x *superbum*	Polaris
Cimicifuga simplex	
Crambe cordifolia	
Delphinium x *belladonna*	
Lilium orientalis	Casablanca
Dicentra spectabilis	Alba
Galliium odoratum	

Botanical Name	Cultivar Name
Galtonia candicans	Summer Hyacinth
Host sp.	Ginkgo Craig
Iris sibirica	White Swirl
Lamiastrum galeobdolon	Herman's Pride
Liatris spicata	Floristan White
Lilium longiflorum	Mount Everest
Lysimachia clethroides	
Narcissus sp.	Ice Wings
Pachysandra terminalis	Variegata
Phlox paniculata	David
Phlox subulata	Bruce White
Polygonatum odoratum	
Sanguinaria canadensis	
Stachys byzantina	Silver Carpet
Tradescantia x *andersoniana*	Snowcap
Valerian officinalis	
Veronica longifolia var. *alba*	
Veronica spicata	Icicle
Vinca minor	Alba

SUGGESTIONS FOR WHITE GARDEN ANNUALS FROM KINGSBRAE GARDEN

Botanical Name
Petunia x *hybrida*
Alyssum maritima procumbens
Cosmos bipinnatus
Cleome spinosa
Nicotiana x *sanderae*
Impatiens walleriana
Begonia semperflorens

Public Gardens

Suggestions for White Garden Trees and Shrubs from Kingsbrae Garden

Botanical Name

Cornus alba
Syringa sp.
Malus
Potentilla fruticosa
Symphoricarpus albus
Hydrangea paniculata

The New Brunswick Botanical Garden
St. Jacques

A wonderful surprise has greeted visitors to the northwestern region of New Brunswick each summer since 1993. That was the first year that the provincial botanical garden was officially opened to the public, in the small village of St. Jacques, eight kilometres from the Québec–New Brunswick border. Planted along the banks of the Madawaska River, just off the Trans-Canada Highway, the New Brunswick Botanical Garden is a seventeen-acre paradise surrounded by rolling hills and mixed forests—a showcase of natural beauty and a source of pride to citizens of the province.

Many New Brunswickers were involved with the planning and construction of this majestic garden. Most of the design, however, was done by landscape architect Michel Marceau of the Montréal Botanical Garden. He did an extensive study of a variety of gardens in both Europe and North America before he began the task of creating the New Brunswick Botanical Garden. Through all of his preparatory work, he maintained a desire to have the garden leave an impression of romance with its visitors. He also wanted a classical yet intimate setting. To this end, he planned a series of eight separate and unique garden rooms, each isolated from the other by lush grassy areas. These rooms have been connected by immaculately edged gravel walking paths so that visitors can stroll from one area to another. And leading to it all is a striking entrance pavilion, the front of which features a vivid collection of thousands of vibrantly coloured geraniums and at least a dozen varieties of annual flowers. Each year, this inviting display forms a sea of bloom to welcome guests into a reception hall where they will find a small gift shop, a licensed restaurant, a comfortable rest area, and an exhibition room.

There are approximately 80,000 plants representing 1,500 species at the New Brunswick Botanical Garden, which provides something for everyone to enjoy. Some visitors prefer the garden's roses—all 850 of them—whose heavenly scent wafts through the air all summer long. Others are impressed with the alpine garden, featured at the top of a rocky outcrop. Cascading down over this collection of boulders and stones, a waterfall flows into a meandering brook that's bordered, at intervals, with iris and daylilies. The water that fills this stream bed is diverted from the nearby river with the aid of special pumps that deliver 600 gallons of water per minute!

Still other garden visitors are fond of the numerous beds of herbaceous perennials, where hundreds of different species are grouped together in ever-changing colour combinations. There is always one variety or other in full bloom, from daylilies to delphiniums and astilbe to asters, and beds are flanked by plantings of native trees and shrubs.

The Botanical Garden is also home to a fine collection of rhododendrons, to an inviting gazebo overlooking a pond filled with floating aquatic plants, and to a fine display of shade-loving perennials. A vegetable garden highlights new varieties, and medicinal herbs emit their individual fragrances. A recycling display allows the environmentally conscious to take a peek inside the garden's numerous model compost units to see just which one they might want to put in their own backyards.

Comfortable benches are scattered throughout the various areas of the garden so weary wanderers can relax and enjoy their surroundings while they rest. Garden visitors might even be lucky enough to hear the soothing strains of a Mozart piano sonata or

The New Brunswick Botanical Garden, in the small village of St. Jacques, is a seventeen-acre paradise surrounded by rolling hills.

the works of Handel, Bach, and Vivaldi, if they are sitting in just the right spot.

Harbour Park
St. Martins

St. Martins is a seaside village where you can enjoy a quiet walk along a picturesque saltwater beach. It's a scenic place with a typical New Brunswick vista of rock cliffs, lighthouses and fishing wharfs. It's a place where you can always find shorebirds in flight, buoys bobbing, and the ocean rising and receding with the famous Bay of Fundy tides. It's also a place where people love to garden. Every summer, local inns and gift shops take time to create gorgeous plant displays for tourists and homecomers to enjoy during their stay in the village; window boxes, hanging baskets, and patio planters provide colour all along the main

Public Gardens

street. Private residences also contribute to the homey setting of the place, giving passers-by a glimpse of backyard vegetable plots, rose hedges, rock gardens, and perennial borders.

In recent years, one the most scenic spots in St. Martins has been right in the heart of the village. There, the St. Martins Beautification Society has been involved, since the early 1980s, in transforming approximately twelve acres of land (donated by the Hearst Corporation) into what is now known as Harbour Park. The area was once the site of an old mill on the village's silt-filled harbour. But after lots of dredging, earth work, and landscaping, the place has become a beautiful garden and recreation area: a picnic spot is surrounded by oaks, red roses, and lilacs; a freshwater swimming beach lies behind a dam on the river that flows into the village; and there is a fish ladder and enclosed observation gallery where visitors can descend into a room at the base of the waterway and see fish working their way upstream. There is the scenic beauty of the Vaughan Creek and Hardscrabble covered bridges, sandstone cliffs topped with old-growth forest, and the village wharf where the local fishing fleet seeks shelter from the sea.

In the centre of it all is a garden that features a marvellous collection of shrubs, trees, herbaceous perennials, and grassy islands surrounding a freshwater and a saltwater pond. The freshwater pond is constantly being fed by a pipe running underground from the waterway behind the fish ladder. The saltwater pond—made by berming an area adjacent to the tidal creek—is inundated by the sea twice daily at high tide. It has been named the "Emerald Pond" because its salty water usually has the typical greenish hue of the nearby ocean. An ornate footbridge has been built over the channel that connects these two bodies of water, and an open-air gazebo has been placed to let garden visitors enjoy the sounds and salt-air smells around them.

Verna and Henry Huttges are local residents who've played an active role in the development of Harbour Park. Verna (president of the St. Martins Beautification Society) is a fine gardener who has contributed many plants to the park from her own home garden. Henry (who is retired from a life's work in construction, landscaping, and lumbering) has been the project manager for all of the work done to create the horticultural garden and its surrounding park features.

Right from the start, the garden's design called for the planting of a wide variety of shrubs and trees. Potentilla, both white and yellow blooming varieties, were chosen because they flower all summer long. Variegated-leaved dogwood and purple-leaved sandcherry were planted for their attractive foliage and colourful red stems that stand out, even in winter. Rhododendrons were selected for their early spring flowers, while sumac and hydrangeas were meant to give a perky display in the fall. Lilacs, spirea, aruncus, weigela, and roses were added for their individual appeal.

Deciduous trees like white and grey birch were planted for their interesting bark colour and rapid growth, evergreens with various needle colours and growth forms complement other woody plants in the collection.

There were also herbaceous perennials placed in various areas around the gardens, including daylilies, hosta, iris, astilbe, and dozens of clumps of Autumn Joy sedum. "We stopped planting annuals a few years ago," admits Henry Huttges, "because we decided that they didn't fit into the natural look that we wanted to portray in the garden."

Along with the desire to create a landscape feature in the village, the St. Martins Beautification Society wanted to help visitors learn about the area's heritage. So, amid the greenery of the garden, near a full-sized lighthouse that serves not only as a reminder of the maritime nature of the setting, but as an information centre for tourists, the Society placed a series of plaques and displays that outline the boat-building history of the village. There is a tribute to Jennie and Ernest Vaughan, who once owned a shipyard in St. Martins, and replicas of vessels constructed by other well-known boat building families including the Morans, the Bradshaws, the Brown-Marrs, and the Carsons.

Henry Huttges has been involved in organizing Society members and community residents in the ongoing upkeep of the St. Martins garden. These volunteers donate time to add fertilizer, prune trees, and weed. "The entire project has become our garden," he says, because the joint effort involved in the garden's creation and continuity have developed a real sense of community spirit in the village.

Fundy Park
Alma

The formal flower beds that grace the landscape around the Headquarters area of Fundy National Park are a drawing card for visitors. They are composed of a series of planting areas, most of which border the roadways near the junction of Route 114 Highway and the Pointe Wolfe Road. Some of these beds are long and rectangular, while others are eyebrow shaped with edges that follow the direction of the road's curbing. Some beds flank the "Fundy Bowl," which is a huge grassy depression with a duck pond at its base; one especially handsome bed sits at the centre of the traffic circle on the road to the golf course clubhouse. From the time they're planted until the fall frosts make their mark, these gardens have an audience of admirers from sun-up to sun-down; here, the click of cameras is a common sound.

The ultimate responsibility for care and management of the gardens and the golf course at Fundy falls to the Park's horticulturist, Rod Lutes. He's a turf expert with many years experience dealing with the upkeep of golf course greens and fairways. And he's also well versed in the challenges associated with gardening in a seaside setting, having lived and worked in Alma for the last fifteen years. Rod and his grounds crew deal with weather conditions ranging from fog and drizzle to intense sun and extended periods of drought, and maintain a landscape in light breezes and full-blown gales. They also find themselves the centre of attention for the many Park visitors touring through the gar-

Fundy Park's gardeners deal with fog and drizzle, sun and drought, and full-blown gales.

dens, and spend lots of time answering questions and posing for photographs beside the flowers that they're tending.

The gardening year at Fundy actually starts in late August when the grounds crew gets together to discuss which plants did well and which ones were obvious problems—either because they couldn't cope with the climate, were prone to diseases or pests, or because they just were not outstanding performers. Based on this review, and on a survey of catalogues for plants that look worth a try, new plant lists are compiled and orders placed for the next summer. Although Fundy used to have on-site greenhouses where bedding plants for the Park were grown, current practice is to have the required number and type of annuals grown by an outside supplier and delivered to the Park in time for planting.

Bed preparation begins each spring, when composted manure and an application of 4-12-8 granular fertilizer is tilled into the soil. Then the beds are sculpted so that soil in their middle section is highest, sloping downwards to the sides. Edging is done just before the beds are planted. "Each member of the grounds crew has their favourite edging tool, ranging from an axe to a half-moon edger or a power edger," says Rod. Edging makes for a manicured look and is a great way to keep the roots of grass and lawn weeds from working their way into flower beds. "There is nothing nicer than a properly-edged flower bed." Midsummer edging is done when touch-ups are needed.

At planting time, annuals are set out based on plant height. "The crew usually picks six or seven different species that they know will grow to a certain height" says Rod, "and plants them down a row, repeating the pattern in the next row with a collection of different plants that are either shorter or taller." For example, there could be alyssum, portulaca, sanvitalia, pansy, ageratum, iceplant, and nieremburgia in one row, and a similar number of slightly-higher species in the next row (such as dwarf aster, dianthus, zinnia, calendula, snapdragon, cosmos, and nasturtium). "The tallest plants are in the middle of the beds," says Rod, "and we work outwards with progressively shorter varieties."

In addition to the mixed colours and species approach, six of the Park's beds are planted with a single type of annual, making for bold displays of identical colours and textures. There might be a mass planting of ornamental tobacco or lavatera, for example. Or there could be an entire bed of annual dahlias. A particularly pleasing combination is a perimeter row of white candytuft around a large number of brilliant, red-flowered geraniums. "The grounds crew try some new combinations each year," says Rod, "but they'll stick with a winning bed of flowering kale, ornamental cabbage, or gloriosa daisies, year after year." It seems that what the grounds crew likes, the public likes, because there are always lots of compliments recorded with park officials.

Insect pests are only a minor concern for the park gardeners, and then only during the few hot days of midsummer. Because he's a firm believer in a natural approach to pest management, and because he's dealing with a public greenspace in a national park, Rod prefers to place sticky strips (made from yellow cardboard covered with a sticky substance that traps bugs) throughout the beds when an infestation is evident. He'll occasionally spray with natural insecticides made of soap-based compounds, and use biological controls for soil nematodes.

As could be expected in a humid coastal climate, fungal diseases like powdery mildew attack the beds at Fundy Park from time to time. "The annuals used to be spaced at six inch (15 cm) intervals, which made for very tight quarters when they were fully grown," says Rod. Tightly-clustered plants have poor air circulation, which is a great environment for fungus. "But we've started spacing the plants farther apart in recent years," he continues, "which has minimized the mildew problem, with very little effect on the fullness of the beds."

In midsummer, when annuals at Fundy are at their peak, they receive additional fertilizer through watering hoses—usually a 20-20-20 formulation, but the grounds crew has also used 15-30-15. This bit of extra nourishment ensures that gardens will remain in full bloom until the majority of park visitors start to pack away their hiking and camping gear and think ahead to winter. It can be as late as Thanksgiving Weekend, however, before the crew begins to pull frost-killed plants out of the beds and to tidy things up until the next season. By then, it's time for the planning session for next year's plants. So goes the cycle of gardening at one of Canada's most beautiful national parks.

Roosevelt International Park
Campobello

Franklin Delano Roosevelt first visited Campobello Island during the summer of 1883. He was just one year old, vacationing with his wealthy New York parents. The Roosevelts so enjoyed their stay that they purchased land on the island and built a summer home. Franklin continued to visit there through the summers of his childhood and into his adult life. Even after he became President of the United States, he continued to refer to Campobello as his "beloved island."

Today, 2,600 acres of Campobello has been made into a park to preserve the memory of this man. The only "International Park" in the world, it was officially opened in the summer of 1964 by Maryon Pearson and Claudia Taylor (Lady Bird) Johnson, the wives of (respectively) Prime Minister Lester Pearson and U.S. President Lyndon B. Johnson. The Queen Mother attended the Park's Visitor's Centre opening, just two years later. Today, the Park is operated under a joint agreement by the governments of the United States and Canada. A special attraction within its boundaries is the original Roosevelt Cottage, which overlooks Friar's Bay on the northeast side of the Island. Both cottage and Visitor's Centre are surrounded by gorgeous gardens which make a summer visit to the Park enjoyable for both history buffs and gardeners alike.

Harold Bailey has worked at the Roosevelt International Park for the last twenty-five years. As head naturalist, he supervises the Park's gardeners and is responsible for establishing and implementing the yearly planting and grounds-maintenance schedule. He begins this work shortly after the gardens are closed each fall, creating detailed garden layouts for the following summer. It's a time consuming process, with many beds to plan: eight beds around the Visitor's Centre, another eight beds near the Roosevelt cottage, and an additional ten beds around other cottages in the Park. There's also a large dahlia bed at the James and Sarah Roosevelt lot in honour of President Roosevelt's parents, and a "replacement garden" where a variety of material is grown as "plants in waiting"—just in case it's necessary to replace something doing poorly in the other beds. All these planting areas, accompanied by hanging baskets, window boxes, and planters, means that wherever you look there are blossoms.

Left to right: Harold Bailey (head naturalist), Christine Riggs (assistant gardener), and Del Dinsmore (head gardener) design and care for the gardens of 2,600-acre Roosevelt International Park.

"American visitors can tell that they're in Canada," says Harold, "because of the emphasis that's put on flowers!"

Some bed designs remain the same each year, so they involve minimum design, but others change annually and have to be planned from scratch. Harold keeps all gardens measurements on file so he can order the correct amount of material to ensure a full display of flowers. And he tries to mix and match interesting bloom colours in his designs, while paying attention to how plant heights fit into the layout.

Once bed designs are completed, Harold places his seed and plant orders. Even though he does keep most of the garden's tuberous begonias over from one year to the next, he regularly requires as many as sixty additional tubers each spring. Dahlias

Public Gardens

are also kept from year to year, but at least 175 new ones are usually on the annual order sheet.

Harold also orders fuchsia cuttings for the many hanging baskets that decorate the Visitor's Centre and cottage porches each summer, and orders large quantities of seeds to grow the annual bedding plants used in the Park's gardens. They regularly include familiar varieties of zinnias, salpiglossis, lobelia, marigolds, snapdragons, wax begonias, verbena, ageratum, dusty miller, asters, pansies, salvia, candytuft, dianthus, and corn flowers. Occasionally Harold orders something new and unusual, just for a change.

When seeds arrive, Harold and the full-time head gardener, Del Dinsmore, start up the Parks' greenhouse facilities. They also establish a planting schedule, so that they know when to start sowing seeds. Geraniums and impatiens are some of the first seeds they start growing because these species take such a long time to reach the blooming stage. By the end of March, all species are underway, and the greenhouse is a very crowded place.

At this stage, Christine Riggs returns to work as assistant Park gardener to help with the ever-increasing number of gardening tasks. When temperatures finally warm and material is hardened off, she and Del start moving plants to the appropriate sites on the Park grounds. It's a big job, but Del has been doing it for twenty-one years and Christine has been helping him for sixteen seasons, so they have a smooth, well-refined system.

Just before they begin transplanting, soil is prepared in the planting beds. First they work in composted sheep manure, and then they till and edge. Some gardens are circular and raised in the centre, while others are long and narrow, their surfaces flush with surrounding lawns. Some gardens are at the foundations of the Visitor's Centre and the Park's cottages, while others highlight the parking area. The fact that gardens are spread over several acres of property means lots of long days for the gardeners at planting time.

Once the beds are created, there are the daily tasks of removing spent blossoms, cultivating the soil surface around the base of each plant to control weeds, keeping the bed edges as straight as an arrow, and watering during extended periods of drought. Liquid fertilizer is applied every two weeks during the growing season to keep the plants healthy and blooming prolifically. But it's more than fertilizer that contributes to the abundance of blossoms. "The plants look as good as they do because the gardeners care so much" says Harold Bailey. Christine, who actually has a greenhouse business of her own that she attends to when not working at Roosevelt Park, never tires of the job. "I'm getting paid to do my hobby," she admits as she reaches down to pinch a drooping begonia flower from the bed at her feet.

Along with routine care and maintenance, gardeners are also involved with visitors. Del and Christine are approached by many people during the run of a day to answer dozens of questions about the gardens at Roosevelt Park. When asked for hints about growing grass—because lawns at the Park are especially lush and green—they explain that no herbicides are used, that lime is applied every year or two, that an application of slow-release lawn fertilizer is made every spring and fall, and that watering is done after a few dry days. When asked about the containers used for the Park's hanging baskets, they explain that these are old, wire, egg-collecting baskets rescued from a local hen farm before it went out of business. The baskets are made of sturdy wire that has been painted a deep green colour; each spring they're lined with moss and planted with an assortment of colourful annuals. The secret to keeping them looking their best all summer lies in never letting them dry out and in supplying them with fertilizer every two weeks.

When Del and Christine are asked about the lilac, the mock orange trees, and the barberry bushes that grow all around the grounds, they reply that these shrubs have been there as long as the Roosevelt cottage. When asked how the beautiful rugosa roses are kept so healthy and vigorous, they describe how the plants are cut back heavily every second season to encourage the growth of productive new stems. The Hybrid Tea roses get a similar pruning treatment. Visitors are often surprised to hear that these tender roses are actually successfully wintered in their beds by having the base of their stems completely mounded over with earth each fall. "We tried to protect them with styrofoam rose cones one winter, but didn't have much success," says Harold, so they now resort to the mounding process after the roses' leaves have dropped in late October or early November.

There are other interesting facts about the gardens that visitors sometimes don't ask about, but that make for great conversation. One might wonder, for example, what is used to stake delphiniums at the front of the Hubbard Cottage. The answer is recycled herring stakes that came from a fisherman in Lubec, Maine. Made from durable hardwood and originally intended to be strung through fillets of herring in a drying shed, they're just the thing for keeping tall and stately delphiniums from collapsing under the weight of their own blossoms.

One might also wonder why there's a "No Entry" sign posted, for a period of time each June, on the gravel walk that runs under a magnificent linden tree behind the Roosevelt cottage. The answer is that the tree is in full bloom at that time, making it a gigantic magnet for bees. That wouldn't be so bad if the bees just kept themselves busy in the tree canopy high above the general public. But park staff have found that the bees help themselves to so much of the sweetness of the linden flowers that they actually get sleepy or "drunk on goodness" and tend to fall to the ground below. Unfortunately, when unsuspecting humans are walking under the tree just when bees happen to be dropping, the result is a stinging hitchhiker landing in open shirt collars. It's not a pleasant thing to happen either for the visitors or for the bees.

Del and Christine are asked a dozen times a day about the sources for the Park's dahlias (some of them produce blooms the size of dinner plates) or the tuberous begonias (which make a splash of colour in a shady spot on the grounds adjacent to the Roosevelt cottage) or the fuchsias (which make some of the Park's hanging baskets worth using an entire role of film to photograph), so they've created a small information sheet with these supplier names and addresses, keeping copies in their uniform pockets for ready dispersal. It's certainly a friendly gesture, and it adds to the overall impression that visitors take from Roosevelt Park at the end of a wonderful day. And that's the impression that staff at this Park strive for—after all, it was the favourite spot of an American President because of this same type of island hospitality in his day!

The Secrets of Public Gardens

- Prepare the soil in planting beds by mixing in composted manure or granular fertilizer
- Edge flower beds to give them a finished look and to keep the roots of grass and other weeds from moving in from the margins
- Keep hanging baskets looking their best by never letting them dry out and by applying plant food every two weeks
- Mix and match colours of annuals, and arrange them in beds according to their height
- Remove spent flowers regularly to keep annuals blooming
- Prune rugosa roses hard, every second year, to encourage the production of new growth

Heritage Gardens

"An heirloom is a valued possession passed down...through successive generations."
The American Heritage Dictionary

The history of gardening in New Brunswick has not been well documented. It's known that a few small vegetable plots were planted on St. Croix Island by the members of Sieur De Mont's expedition in 1604, but the settlement and gardens were abandoned after a single Canadian winter caused many members of the expedition to perish.

Other explorers and colonists arrived in the province, and with them came seeds and agricultural implements necessary for cultivating the land. The focus of the earliest gardens would have been food production, of course, and the need for vigorous, disease-resistant crop plants, with varieties that would mature in a short growing season. Wildflowers would have provided the only bouquets, until farmers were prosperous enough to devote effort to plants that weren't utilitarian, or until wealthy landowners started to grow some ornamentals around their property. It became the height of fashion, then, to have colourful perennials and exotic annuals gracing the yards of some of New Brunswick's more illustrious homes.

Today, remnants of some of these old-fashioned plants still grow in abandoned homestead gardens, in ancient apple orchards, and in overgrown farm fields. These are heirlooms, rugged and persistent enough to survive neglect and the ravages of time. Heirloom plants are also found in the heritage gardens at King's Landing Historical Settlement and at the Village Historique Acadien. In these historic settings, plants are used to illustrate why and how our ancestors gardened.

Village Historique Acadien
Caraquet

Running along the Rivière-du-Nord, near the town of Caraquet in northeastern New Brunswick, the Village Historique Acadien is a living museum that portrays Acadian life in the province between 1770 and 1890. The Village's main focus is to illustrate the activities of an industrious people, who worked hard to survive in a difficult time and place.

Sylvain Godin, the site's chief historian, explains that the Acadians were both fishers and farmers, but that "they had no time for gardening with flowers." The only blossoms adding beauty to the landscape at the Village Historique Acadien are naturally-occurring wildflowers like buttercups, goldenrod, fireweed, tansy, and native roses; the cultivated gardens and fields are restricted to crop plants grown to provide produce for the kitchen, or for livestock feed. These gardens are planted to show how Acadians maintained self-sufficiency by adapting to the limitations of the land, and their beauty lies in their simplicity.

Acadians came to New Brunswick from rural regions of France in the mid 1600s and farmed in the area for almost a century, using agricultural methods brought from their native France. Between 1755 and 1759, they were forced from their land by the English, in what is now known as "The Great Expulsion." In this tragic time, Acadians were dispersed along the eastern coast of North America. However, by 1763 political tensions had eased, and the Acadians began to return to some of their homesteads along the shores of New Brunswick and Nova

Caraquet's Village Historique Acadien portrays Acadian life in the province between 1770 and 1890. Its only blossoms are naturally-occurring wildflowers, but outside almost every house are vegetable gardens.

dot the marshlands at the Village Historique Acadien, where modern-day visitors can appreciate this unique farming technique.

Flax was another crop usually grown on the marshes, but at the Village it's planted in a more accessible plot on the Cyr Farm, at the front of the house. The flax plot has been surrounded by a typical Acadian-style log fence that is self-supporting, without nails or wire holding it together, so that it can be easily dismantled at harvest time.

Outside almost every house at the Village Historique Acadien are vegetable gardens. Near the Doucet Farm, restored to the 1860s, is a large garden of long, hilled rows full of potatoes, turnips, and cabbage, all of which would have been harvested for winter storage in a root cellar. Beside the 1770 Martin House, a log cabin in a wooded part of the Village, grows a much smaller garden where potatoes, turnips, and broad beans are planted, surrounded by a twig fence to keep vegetables safe from hungry wildlife. And at the Robichaud Farm, which represents the 1825 home of an Acadian who had returned from exile, there are enough potatoes, peas, turnips, and broad beans to feed the family of twelve that would have made up this Acadian household.

In other Village gardens, potatoes, turnips, and cabbage grow alongside onions, beets, and parsnips. "These were all crops suited for growing in New Brunswick," relates Sylvain, "and the types of vegetables that were best for long-term storage." "But we

Scotia. They struggled to feed themselves, living by the sea. They didn't clear large tracts of forest to make land for cultivation, but turned, instead, to marshes at the mouths of rivers and to sheltered coves and bays. These areas had rich, fertile soil that had to be drained for agriculture. Building a system of dykes and levees ("aboiteaux"), Acadians reclaimed marshland for crops.

According to Sylvain Godin, Acadiens harvested native grasses and grew crops like wheat, barley, oats, and buckwheat on the drained marshes. "They also constructed elevated wooden racks on the marsh, in which they stored the harvest from these forage crops until freeze-up." A series of aboiteaux and hayracks can find no evidence that carrots were grown in Acadian gardens after the expulsion," he admits. So, although people think of carrots as an old-fashioned root vegetable, these have been deliberately left out of the Village gardens. The fact that each garden grows potatoes is also no accident; potatoes were planted in great numbers, and are still used in typical Acadian foods such as fricot and poutine rapé.

The only fruit tree grown by Acadians was the apple, so apple trees are scattered all about the Village. Wild blueberries, cranberries, raspberries, and strawberries were also harvested and preserved. There was no need to grow these fruit in a garden when they grew in abundance on their own.

To add nutrients to the soil before planting their gardens, Acadians worked in manure, herring, and other fish waste, including the shells of lobster and crab. "Acadians also had faith in mud as a fertilizer" relates Sylvain. The mud was dug from mussel beds on the shore and transported to gardens with teams of oxen. "Horses were too expensive to feed," says Sylvain, "so oxen were the farm beasts of choice for Acadians."

The same farmers have worked many years at the Village Historique Acadien, planting and caring for all of its gardens. They use horses now, rather than oxen, and for fertilizer they stick to manure from animals kept on site, rather than fish waste or mussel mud. But their role at the village is otherwise an exact replica of their Acadian ancestors, and their work helps us remember that gardening was a vital part of life in Acadie.

King's Landing Historical Settlement
Prince William

A walk through King's Landing's gardens is a walk through the history of New Brunswick's cultivated plants, and an opportunity to admire some of the heirloom species grown by earlier residents of New Brunswick.

As described in an earlier chapter ("Herbs"), King's Landing Historical Settlement is in Prince William, approximately 40 km west of Fredericton. Here, a collection of eleven gardens has been created to reflect what planting would have been like in the province during the nineteenth century. These gardens grow outside historic homes restored to the 1820-1890 era, and are planted with heritage varieties carefully researched by King's Landing's head gardener, Ruth Lefevre. Over the years she has identified sources of seeds, tubers, or root stocks known to be grown in New Brunswick at the time of the Loyalists. With the help of Neil Carson, the Settlement's assistant gardener, Ruth has created gardens that help visitors learn more about the life of the people of that time and place. Dressed in period costume and usually carrying woven baskets and hoes, these two heritage gardeners take great pride in keeping weeds at bay and in answering questions from curious King's Landing visitors.

Ruth begins each growing season by starting seeds that she's either saved from the previous year's harvest, or purchased from seed houses that specialize in heirloom varieties. She grows these in the King's Landing greenhouse and cold frame, so they're ready for transplanting at the beginning of the garden season. Then, depending on the time period represented at each house in the Settlement, she prepares a historically-appropriate planting plan that dictates where specific types of vegetables, flowers, and herbs are to be placed.

In the 1820s garden at the home of Daniel Morehouse, for example, visitors can find a heritage lettuce known as Deer Tongue and the heritage cabbage Early Jersey Wakefield. These vegetables are joined by a variety of corn with white kernels, the type available before more modern, yellow-kernelled varieties. Then there are China Rose radishes, which have been in cultivation for hundreds of years, and rambling West India Gherkin cucumbers, which produce an abundance of small, oval fruit for tasty and unusual-looking pickles. Chioggia beets are an Italian heirloom variety, and Jenny Lind melons are known to be the sweetest melons around.

All of these interesting vegetables are surrounded by a sturdy wooden fence, which would have been built to keep free-roaming

Dressed in period costume, Ruth Lefevre and Neil Carson take great pride in keeping weeds at bay at King's Landing Historical Settlement.

farm animals from invading the harvest. Closer to the back door of the house is a herb garden with age-old varieties like sage, comfrey, wormwood, mint, chamomile, marjoram, horseradish, and tansy. The Settlement staff makes great use of these plants when showing visitors how salves, ointments, and dyes were made over a century ago.

For flower lovers, a trip to the Ingraham house gardens is a real treat. Here, a formal planting design represents the garden of a wealthy 1840s landowner, and features four raised beds around a quaint and functional sundial. It's a mass of colour from heritage flower varieties of both annual and perennial species—love-lies-bleeding, amaranthus, cosmos, celosia, zinnias, alyssum, marigolds, asters, pansies, purple coneflowers, delphiniums, and rudbeckia, to list just a few. These plant names might sound modern, but have been cultivated by gardeners for a century or more. There are a number of old-fashioned rose bushes, lilacs, mock orange bushes, apple trees, and a grape arbour in this heritage garden.

In addition to the Settlement's heirloom garden plants, there are historically-appropriate arable crops growing in the farm fields. A large field of buckwheat is planted, harvested, and then ground into flour at the Settlement's grist mill each fall. Another field is planted with flax, used by Loyalists for cloth production. Several fields of oats and barley are harvested to feed some of the Settlement's animals, and plots of turnips, pumpkin, and squash would have been collected for winter storage in the root cellars of Loyalist farms.

As each summer progresses, the vegetables and fruit that grow at King's Landing are gathered and preserved by Settlement staff for use at the King's Head Inn throughout the winter. As another season of growing heirlooms comes to a close, harvesting is done in much the same way as it was in the nineteenth century; flower and grain seeds are collected and stored for the next year's crop, perpetuating their genetic contribution to the province's gardening history.

The Secrets of Heritage Gardens

- Consult the provincial archives (or historians at places like King's Landing and the Village Historique Acadien) in order to determine what plants are considered part of New Brunswick's heritage.
- Use organic fertilizers in your planting beds because this is all that was available to Loyalists and Acadiens.
- Choose root crops like potatoes and turnips, and storage vegetables like cabbage and broad beans.
- Put fences around your garden to keep out deer or stray animals.
- Collect seeds in the fall to maintain your heritage varieties from year to year.

Steve Stehouwer, McLeod Hill

Seed Savers

"The gardener who saves seeds from this year's crop to plant in next year's garden has, in addition to the assurance that he or she is prepared for the future, the prospect of experiment, discovery, even surprise."

Nancy Bubel

There are many benefits to saving seeds from plants grown in your garden. First, it allows you to keep a bit of money in your pocket, because the annual order that you send off to the seed house will be that much shorter. Second, it's a way for you to make sure that the seeds you plant each year haven't been treated with any type of pesticide (assuming you've kept such products out of your own garden while seeds were being formed). Third, it's a way for you to share some of your favourite plants with friends and neighbours, in a seed exchange. And, finally, it's the process by which old-fashioned types of vegetables and flowering plants can be perpetuated. These "heritage plants" aren't commonly found in seed catalogues anymore; they're most often open-pollinated varieties rather than hybrids. This means that they have not been subjected to breeding programs and repeated hybridizing processes, which tend to restrict gene pools over time. By constantly choosing hybrids, the world runs the risk of losing some of its genetic diversity. It's worrisome to think that if at least some gardeners or farmers don't continue to sow and harvest seeds each year, there's a chance that the time will come when some of our most valued food plants and ornamentals will no longer be available. Luckily the following gardeners have already taken up the challenge.

Steve Stehouwer
McLeod Hill

The end of the gardening season is an important time for Steve Stehouwer. It's not that he doesn't enjoy the spring, when he prepares hundreds of transplants for placement in his flower and vegetable plots. And it's not that he isn't content with summer months spent weeding, pruning, and mowing around the gardens that spread over his property—sometimes up to twenty hours a week. It's just that, in the autumn, Steve can spend time at his favourite garden activity: collecting seeds.

During the waning days of the season, he does the bulk of his gathering. Equipped with containers and marking pens and a mental list of the plants in his collection from which he needs to save seeds, he spends a great deal of time picking, labelling, and sorting the seeds produced from the many plants under his care. Some seeds are too moist to be stored right away and have to be dried on sheets of newspaper or towelling, so that they don't get covered with mold. Others need to be frozen for several months in order for their dormancy period to be broken. But many of the seeds that Steve collects are dry when picked, and only need to be gathered into paper envelopes and stored in a cool, dry location until planting time. For this avid seed collector, the work is worth it. "Gardening is something to be shared," he says, and what better way to do so than to pass along seeds.

This interest in seed collecting probably began with his first garden. Several years ago, when Steve and his wife Annette arrived in Fredericton, they moved into a new home that needed some colour in the backyard. Starting with a modest number of annuals, then adding herbs and perennials the next season, Steve soon realized just how much he loved to grow things and how much he enjoyed working with plants. He was hooked on gardening and began meeting others who shared the same affliction. These people gave him gifts of plants and seeds, and inspired him to begin collecting and propagating his own material so that he could return their generosity. When he and his family moved to a three-acre property at the top of McLeod Hill, he began to garden in earnest, creating what he now calls "a work in progress." To date, he has produced a unique landscape where hundreds of varieties of plants thrive. It's a place where there is always room for something different. And it's where Steve's seed collecting has taken on a new intensity. As he learns about sources for new types of plants, and as he acquires seeds of novel plant varieties from collectors all over the world, he prepares new planting beds and display gardens. The design is simple, based on a continuous need to expand. Dozens of individual plots are surrounded by lawn. "It's all stretched out" he says, but there's a place for everything to grow, prosper, and produce seed.

Take the perennials, for example. Last spring, Steve started 170 different perennials from seed. He grew them in his lean-to style greenhouse, germinating seeds in plastic 500 ml margarine tubs, and transplanting them into various types of nursery pots or trays. When the seedlings were ready to be hardened off, he moved them to his sheltered patio, where they stayed until planting time. (Extras were given to a charitable plant sale, or to friends and neighbours.) His new seedlings joined hundreds of novel varieties of lilies, dephiniums, flowering onions, beebalm, daylilies, primroses, hostas, and more. Steve also grows a hardy cactus, which survives a New Brunswick winter as if it was a native. He has alpine plants grown from seed supplied by a fellow rock-gardener, along with herbs, bulbs, ground cover plants, and hardy climbers. A clematis and a bittersweet vine battle it out for wall space at the side of the house, while a Valiant variety of grape provides as much as 30 lb of fruit each year. And raspberry canes of the Titan variety also have a place in his garden.

Then there are the shrubs and trees, many of which Steve grew from seed collected in the wild or from other gardeners. His Hope for Humanity rose is a new release developed to honour the work of the Red Cross, and he has a wonderful new lilac variety called Sensitive, with wine-coloured flowers, each edged with a line of pure white. He grows "half-high" blueberries (a hybrid between high and low bush varieties), tree peonies, honeysuckle, heritage varieties of apple trees, and a large number of native evergreens, which surround the property as a green privacy screen.

On top of all this, Steve also grows vegetables; his sons help him with the seed sowing and enjoy harvesting tasty treats throughout the summer. Steve wants them to know that "plants are a gift and a wonder of nature."

A visitor to the Stehouwer garden can't help but be impressed with the diversity of its plant collection. But it's also hard to miss the intense passion with which its owner approaches the botanical world. Able to reel off a plant's Latin name in a second, always willing to give growing advice and information on seed sources, Steve Stehouwer is committed to his love of gardening and to collecting seeds—a hobby worth cultivating.

Kim Edmondson
Keswick Ridge

"It all started with a handful of calendula seeds!" This simple statement might sound like the opening line of a nursery tale or a whimsical claim in a gardener's planting diary, but it's just the way that Kim Edmondson starts the story of how her business idea became a reality. Five years old, Hope Seeds and Perennials is a small seed company and perennial plant nursery that Kim operates from her home on Keswick Ridge. It's now a

Tomato and cucumber seeds have to go through a fermentation process before they can be dried and packaged (see page 122).

into her heritage. They made her realize that in order for there to be "hope for the future,"—particularly for her children, but also for the global community—the world's gardeners and farmers would have to continue to collect and preserve seeds. That's why she chose the name "Hope Seeds." It seemed to fit her philosophy on life, and her wishes for the years to come.

Kim is an organic grower. When she first started gardening over a decade ago, she wanted to ensure that her children would always be able to play and plant in the garden, and eat its crops. She began by researching environmentally-friendly growing methods and the value of composting, green manure crops, and crop rotation. She became a member of Seeds of Diversity Canada, a group dedicated to preserving old-fashioned, open-pollinated vegetables and flowering plants, and to sharing seeds of these varieties with growers all over the nation. Kim also made herself familiar with the recommendations of Marc Rogers (author of *Saving Seeds: the Gardener's Guide to Growing and Storing Vegetable and Flower Seeds*). It's a book with basic, down-to-earth information about when, where, and how to collect seeds from plants that you want to keep growing year after year. Some plants have great disease resistance, winter hardiness, and tolerance to drought; some grow in marginal soils or produce beautiful fragrant blossoms. But some of them just have an interesting story to tell, because they have been passed down from generation to generation, or exchanged between countries and continents.

It's the story or the catchy name that often gives Kim Edmonson a reason for wanting to collect and propagate a plant at her nursery. For example, she has been given beans called Gilmore Wonder, planted and nurtured for many years in the Gilmore family gardens around Keswick, New Brunswick. She has White Wonder tomatoes that produce yellow fruit and that can be traced back to the 1880s. She grows Charentais muskmelon, an old french heirloom variety. She has Cushaw squash, an interesting type of summer squash with a striped green-and-white peel and a mellow, sweet flavour. She has Rouge Vif d'Etampes pumpkin, which is red, rather than orange, and which

venture that involves the production of at least 30 varieties of unique vegetable and flower seeds, all of which are listed in a yearly catalogue she prepares on her home computer—but the whole thing actually began when Kim's grandmother gave her a few calendula seeds to grow. Because these seeds produced perky, yellow-blossomed plants that reseeded themselves prolifically all over her garden, Kim was annually reminded of how they fit is affectionately called the "Cinderella pumpkin" because it's shaped much like the coach that Cinderella rode to her evening at that magical ball.

Kim also has different types of potatoes, many of which she has collected and propagated in conjunction with the staff at King's Landing Historical Settlement in Prince William, New Brunswick, where she is a research associate. These potatoes, with names like Yam, Forty-fold, and Lumper, came to the province with the Loyalists and have a heritage that can be traced back to Ireland at the time of the potato famine. Their unique skin colour and odd shapes look startlingly different from the modern-day Yukon Gold or Russet Burbank.

Hope Seeds are collected all summer long, when the plants that produce them reach the proper stage of maturity. Depending on the variety and the recommended extraction technique, Kim prepares the results of her seed-gathering sessions for long-term storage. Tomato and cucumber seeds, for example, have to go through a fermentation process before they can be dried and packaged. Bean seeds have to be harvested before they actually germinate in the plant's pods and loose their viability.

Before each seed type is ready for the storage shelf and subsequently listed in the Hope Seeds annual catalogue, Kim performs a germination test so that she is able to give her customers a quality guarantee. She gets all of this work completed as early in the winter as possible, in order to have up-to-date information for her catalogue.

From just a few calendula seeds, a gardener's interest grew. Since her first garden, Kim has continued to learn about the methods and the value of saving seeds. During the process she has become a steward of some interesting heritage varieties. Isn't it comforting to know that someone is trying to look after our plant heritage here in New Brunswick?

The Secrets of Saving Seeds

- Collect seeds after they have ripened, but just before they are mature enough to either drop to the ground or get blown away by wind.
- Tie a well-ventilated paper bag over the seed heads of those ornamental plants that tend to scatter seeds the minute they ripen.
- Label all seeds with the date of collection and the plant's name.
- Keep seeds from getting wet after the initial drying.
- Store seeds in an appropriate place, after they are thoroughly dried.
- Share your seeds with friends and neighbours interested in seed saving.

The Fermentation Process for Cucumber and Tomato Seeds

- Split the fruit and scrape out the surrounding seeds and the pulp.
- Place the mixture in an open glass bowl, and let it sit to ferment in a warm location for a week, stirring daily to keep mould from forming on the surface.
- Collect seeds that have separated from the pulp and settled to the bottom of the bowl.
- Discard the pulp and any seeds that were floating.
- Wash the saved seeds in lukewarm water.
- Spread these seeds on a paper towel, separating them as much as possible.
- Move seeds about periodically, to ensure even drying.
- Gather the (completely) dry seeds and store in a closed container or envelope, in a cool and dry location.

Compost—A Gardener's Best Friend

Does your garden have a compost bin or pile? If not, why not consider starting one this year? After all, there are few negative things to be said about this activity. When done properly, composting is easy and rewarding. It diverts organic matter from the bags of garbage you put out for roadside pickup each week, making your local landfill last longer. It produces a nutrient-rich material that improves soil texture, pH, aeration, and moisture-holding capacity. In fact, this simple choice to compost has many satisfying and beneficial environmental consequences. You can think of people who compost as being stewards of their own small corner of the earth!

In Latin, the word "compost" means "to bring together." This suggests that a healthy compost pile is just a repository for a collection of organic materials. However, the thousands of microorganisms that actually create compost from these organic materials need four main things. First, there must be a source of carbon to provide energy. Carbon-rich compost ingredients include fibrous plant materials like leaves, straw, wood shavings, or sawdust; these materials are called the "browns" of composting.

Second, there must be a source of nitrogen to provide protein. Animal manure, freshly mowed grass, garden refuse, coffee grounds, egg shells, fruit or vegetable peelings, seaweed, and human hair are all great sources of nitrogen. These are referred to as the "greens" of composting.

In addition to nitrogen and carbon, microorganisms in an effective compost pile need two more basic ingredients: oxygen and water. When there is too little oxygen, the pile will begin to give off a bad odour. And when there is too little water, the composting process dramatically slows down.

Finished, usable compost can be produced quickly if you combine the greens and browns in your compost pile in a 1:1 ratio by weight. The pile must be kept moist to the touch and turned once a week (so that what was initially on the bottom moves to the top, and vice versa). And materials should be chopped, shredded, or cut into small pieces. This sort of "pile management" means that composting microorganisms will have ideal conditions in which to live and work. They'll perform their jobs amazingly well, giving off lots of heat in the process. These elevated temperatures kill off pathogens, weed seeds, and disease. This moist, warm, active approach is referred to as the "hot composting method."

However, a compost pile can also be low maintenance. Just keep adding whatever organic matter you have on hand into the compost bin, in any ratio or amount. If you begin to notice an odour, add more carbon-rich material. If you see fruit flies swarming over the compost's surface, cover the top of the pile with a layer of soil. If there seems to be little decomposition going on, add a bit of nitrogen-rich material and some water. This low-key approach to composting is referred to as "the cold composting method." It takes a little longer to produce the final product, but it's still a worthwhile activity.

INDEX

Acadian gardens *see* Village Historique Acadien
ageratum, 39
Alexander, Murray, 29, 30
Allair, Wilma, 87, 88, 89
Alma, 95, 97, 107, 108
Alpine plants, 86, 87
alyssum, 83
American elm, 39
anise hyssop, 80
annuals, 40-49
apple, 39, 58-60
arbour, 20 *see also* border
artemesia, 49
ash, 39
asparagus, 70
astilbe, 5, 83
August lily hosta, 35 *see also* hosta
autumn joy sedum, 5, 91
baby's breath, 5, 49
Bailey, Harold, 109, 110
Baldwin, Deanna, 32, 34
balloon flower, 5
barberry bush, 82
basil, 70, 74, 75, 76, 80 *see also* recipes
basket of gold, 91
Bathurst, 26-28, 97-99
bearberry, 91
bearded iris, 5, 27
beauty bush, 29
bedrock, 32
beebalm, 5, 39, 70, 80
beet, 70
bellflower, 91
birdbath, 31; feeder, 31, 32
black plastic mulch, 65, 69 *see also* mulch
black-eyed Susan, 5
bleeding heart, 5, 83

blooming order of popular perennials, 5 *see also* perennials
border: arbours, 20; boundaries 10, 11; cedar hedge, 23-24, 25-26; cotoneaster hedge, 27; fences, 20, 28, 116, 117; garden dividers, 20; stone walls, 2
Boyce Farmer's Market, 64, 76
Boyd, Dalbert and Margie Ann, 51-53
broccoli, 39, 70
Bt, 65 *see also* pesticide
bugle weed, 5
bulbs, 26, 29, 30, 34, 120
buttercup 5
butterfly: bush, 39, 83; garden, 38-39; plants for, 39; weed, 5 *see also* perennials
cabbage, 39
Calder, Dale, 13-14
calendula, 44
calla lily, 96-97
Cambridge, 74, 75
Campobello, 13, 14, 87, 89, 108, 111
Canada lily, 5
candied flowers, 49
candytuft, 30
canes, 54 *see also* raspberries
capping, 8, 9, 17 *see also* roses
Caraquet, 113-115
Carlow, 28-29, 46-48
carrot, 39, 70
Carson, Neil, 116
caterpillar, 38, 39 *see also* butterfly garden
cedar: fence, 28; hedge 2, 23-24, 25-26 *see also* border
celery, 70
chamomile, 80
cherry, 39
chervil, 80
chive, 80
chlorine, 96 *see also* water gardens
clematis, 5, 13, 14, 49; golden, 13-14; Jackman, 13
cockscomb flower, 47
columbine, 5, 83

124   *Garden Secrets*

common lantana, 39
companion planting, 63-64, 70, 73
compost, 16, 20, 21, 23, 26, 28, 33, 42, 47, 52, 54, 55, 57, 69, 89, 103, 104, 121, 123 *see also* manure, fertilizer
coral bells, 5
Corey, Beverly, 45-46
coriander, 80
corn, 70
Corn Hill, 53-55
cornflower, 39
corydalis, 91
cosmos, 39, 44
cotoneaster: creeping, 5; hedge, 27; rock-spray, 91 *see also* border
cottage pink, 5
Covered Bridge Gardens, 93-95
cranesbill, 5
creeping cotoneaster, 5 *see also* cotoneaster
creeping Jenny, 5
creeping juniper, 5, 91
creeping loosestrife, 37, 38 *see also* loosestrife
creeping mother of thyme, 5
crocus, 25
Cronk, Marilyn and Peter, 66-68
crop rotation, 65, 67, 69
cucumbers, 70
daffodils, 83
dame's rocket, 83
dandelion, 39
daphne, 14-15 *see also* February daphne, trees and shrubs
daylily, 2, 4, 21, 22, 23, 28, 29, 33; tawny, 5
deadheading, 35, 43, 44, 48
deer, 67, 68, 82, 83
deer-resistant plants, 83
delphinium, 49, 83; stakes, 111
devil's walking stick, 14
dill, 70, 80
Dinsmore, Del, 110-111
Douglas, 51-53
dried seeds, 122 *see also* seeds
drying flowers, 48, 49
dwarf papyrus, 98
edible annuals, 49 *see also* annuals
Edmondson, Kim, 120-122
Egyptian onion, 30
Erb, Howard and Marilyn, 74-75

Everett, Fred and Kit, 10-13
fantail goldfish, 96 *see also* goldfish
February daphne, 14-15 *see also* daphne
fences, 20, 28, 82, 116, 117 *see also* border
fennel, 70
fermentation process for cucumber and tomato seeds, 122
fertilizer, 16, 23; granular, 23, 107, 111; nitrogen, 25; slow-release, 97
feverfew, 80
fiddlehead ferns, 24
fish, 94, 96, 99 *see also* goldfish
flax, 70, 114
forsythia, 15, 83
fortune's hosta, 35 *see also* hosta
four-arm kniffin system, 54 *see also* pruning
foxgloves, 83
Fredericton Backyard Compost Committee, 64
Fredericton Garden Club, 42
Fredericton, 56, 57, 58, 89, 90, 91
Frog Lake, 64, 65
fruit, 50-61; recipes, 60-61
Fundy National Park, 95, 107-108
Garden Gate Nursery, 46-48
garlic, 70
gayfeather, 5
geranium, 5, 49; scented, 83
Gibson, Madeline, 21-23
globe thistle, 5
Godin, Sylvain, 113
golden clematis, 13-14 *see also* clematis
goldenrod, 39, 49
goldfish, 96, 99; fantail goldfish, 96
goldmoss stonecrop, 91
gooseneck loosestrife, 37 *see also* loosestrife
grafting, 58, 59, 60 *see also* apples
Grand Falls, 25-26, 31-32
Grand Manan, 66-68
grapes, 11, 12, 53, 54, 55, 59
grass, 110
green manure crops, 69
H. Erb's Herbs, 74-75
Halifax Seed Company, 75
hanging basket, 46, 110, 111
Harbour Park, 105-107
hardiness zone, vi-vii
hedge, 25; candytuft, 30, 91; cedar, 2, 23-24, 25-26; cotoneaster, 27

Index

hens and chickens, 21, 91
herb garden, 4, 32, 33, 117 *see also* herbs
herb recipes, 75, 78 *see also* herbs
herbs for New Brunswick gardens, 80
herbs, 73, 81
heritage gardens, 112-117; apples, 60; from seed, 119
Himalayan balsam, 45, 46
Hinds, Hal, 89-91
hollyhock, 5, 36, 39
Hope Seeds and Perennials, 120-122 *see also* seeds
horseradish, 70
hosta, 27, 35-36
Hovey, Kim, 28-29
Hunter, Daryl, 58- 60
Huttges, Henry and Verna, 106-107
hybrid tea roses, 8, 110-111; edible petals, 49
impatiens, 22
insect, 23, 38, 67, 70, 108
iris, 4, 20-21, 83 *see also* bearded iris
Island View, 8-10
Jacksonville, 43-45
Jacob's ladder, 5
Japanese iris, 94
Japanese primose, 5
Japanese spurge, 5
Joe-Pye weed, 39
Johnny jump-ups, 91
Kerria, 14
Keswick Ridge, 58-60, 120-122
King's Landing Historical Settlement, 75-78, 115-117
Kingsbrae Horticultural Garden, 101-104
Kingston, 78-80
kiwi, 51, 53
kohlrabi, 70
lady's mantle, 5, 49
lamb's ears, 82
lamium, 5
Landauer, Erwin, 86-87
larkspur, 49
lath house, 24
lavatera, 22, 44
lavender, 5, 49, 80, 83
Lefevre, Ruth, 116
lemon balm, 80
lemon beebalm, 22

lemon thyme, 34
leopard's bane, 5
lilac, 2, 15, 28, 39, 83
lily, 3, 15, 28-29; Canada lily, 5; plantain lily, 5; water lily, 96 *see also* daylily, hosta
lily-of-the-valley, 5
liner, 94, 96, 97, 99 *see also* water gardens
Long, Beatrice and Reno, 25-26
loosestrife, 37, 38
lovage, 70, 80
Love, Darlene, 78-80
love-lies-bleeding, 49
Lower St. Mary's, 3-4
Loyalists, 115, 122
lungwort, 5
lupine, 5, 39
Lutes, Rod, 95-97, 107
MacFarlane, Elizabeth, 1-3
manure, 64, 69, 111 *see also* compost
Marceau, Michel, 104
marigold, 22, 41, 70; marsh, 98; petals, 49
marjoram, 80
Marr, Valerie, 77-78
McCoy, Annette and Byron, 3-4
McLeod Hill, 119-120
McMackin, Betty and Jake, 8-9
medicinal herbs, 80 *see also* herbs
Michaelmas daisy, 5, 39
Miller, Don, 9
Miller, John and Lola, 97-99
mint, 78, 80, 83
monkshood, 5, 82
mother of thyme, 91
Mouth of Keswick, 75, 77
mulch, 35, 48; black plastic, 65, 69
Nashwaaksis, 41, 43
nasturtium, 39, 41, 48, 49, 70
New Brunswick Botanical Garden, The, 104-105
New Maryland, 1-3
nigella, 49
obedient plant, 5
onion, 30, 70
oregano, 80
organic fertilizer, 16, 25, 103, 117
organic gardens: fruit, 51-53, 55-56; herbs, 74-75; perennials, 23-25; rock gardens 89-91; seeds, 120-122; vegetables, 63-64, 64-65, 65-68

organic matter, 3, 24, 42, 54, 55, 67, 69, 70, 90, 102, 123
oriental poppy, 5
Osborne, Bob, 53-55
Othello rayflower, 5
overwintering, 9, 17, 23, 34, 35, 94, 95, 99
pansy, 49
paper birch, 39s
parsley, 70, 80
peas, 70
Peck, Ken, 55-56
penstemon, 5
peony, 5, 20, 49, 83
perennials, 1, 4, 5, 12, 18-39; groundcover, 5; order of bloom, 5; "white garden" perennials, 103
periwinkle vine, 5
pesticide, 47, 69; Bt, 65; environmentally friendly, 22 *see also* organic gardens
pests, 108
pH level, 42
phlox, 39
plantain lily, 5
plantain, 39
plum, 39
polaris, 103
pole beans, 70
polyantha primose, 5
poplar, 39
poppy, 49, 83
portulaca, 21
potato, 70
potentilla, 83
powdery mildew, 30, 108
primrose, 90
primula, 90, 91
Prince William 68-70, 75-78, 115-117
pruning, 7, 15, 16, 53, 54, 60; four-arm kniffin system, 54
public gardens, 100-111
pumpkin, 70
purple coneflower, 5, 39
purple loosestrife, 37 *see also* loosestrife
pussytoes, 5
Queen Anne's Lace, 39
Queen-of-the-meadow, 5
Quispamsis, 23-25
radish, 70
Randall, Aaron and Anna, 75-77

raspberry, 55-56
recipes: asparagus and new potato salad with sugar snap peas, 71: basil cheddar crisps, 76-77; broccoli salad, 71; candied flowers, 49; curried carrot soup, 71; favourite fruit recipes, 60-61; fruit pizza with kiwi, 60-61; garden vegetable stuffing for salmon, 70; grape jelly, 61; marinated tomato slices with fresh basil, 75; mint tea, 78; peanut butter apple crumble, 61; pesto, 75; strawberry salad, 61; environmentally, friendly pesticide, 22; rose petal jelly, 16; rosemary hair rinse, 80
red clover, 39
red oiser dogwood, 39
Remay, 67
renovation process, 56, 60
rhizomes, 77
rhododendron, 9-10
Richard, Diane, 31-32
Riggs, Christine, 110-111
rock candytuft, 5
rock cress, 5
rock garden plants for New Brunswick, 91 *see also* rock gardens
rock gardens, 27, 84-91
Rock Garden Societies, 86
rockery plants, 89 *see also* rock gardens
rocket rayflower, 5
rock-spray cotoneaster, 91
rodgersia, 21
Roosevelt International Park, 108, 111
root crops, 117
root stock, 58; *see also* apples
rose cap, 8
rose daphne, 91
rose, 8, 9, 15-17, 33, 49, 83, 101, 110, 111
rosemary, 76, 79, 80; rosemary hair rinse, 80
Rothesay, 9-10
rudbeckia, 83
rue, 70
rugosa rose, 83, 110, 111 *see also* rose
sage, 70, 80, 83
scarlet runner beans, 44
scion wood, 58 *see also* apple
secrets of gardening: annuals, 46; fruit, 60; garden landscape, 4; herbs, 80; New Brunswick heritage plants, 117; perennials, 34, 35; public gardens, 111; rock gardens, 91; saving seeds, 122; trees and shrubs, 17; vegetables, 70; water gardens, 99
seed collecting, 43, 44, 115, 117, 118-122
seed savers, 118-122 *see also* seed collecting

Seeds of Diversity Canada, 121
seersucker hosta, 35; *see also* hosta
shasta daisy, 5, 39
Shepherd's Garden, The, 64, 65
shirley poppy, 42
shrubs *see* trees and shrubs
Sisson Ridge, 86-87
slugs, 36
snapdragon, 49, 83
sneezeweed, 5
sneezewort, 23
soapwort, 91
soil: compacted, 28, 34, 42, 54, 68; cover crops, 102; herbs, 74, 80-81; pH levels, 42
    see also compost, fertilizer, organic matter
spiderwort, 5
spirea, 39
spring flowering shrubs, 14-15
squash, 70
St. Andrews, 101-104
St. George, 93-95
St. Jacques, 104-105
St. John's Wort, 5
St. Martins Beautification Society, 106
St. Martins, 105-107
St. Stephen, 21, 23
Stehouwer, Steve 119-120
Stephenson, Stephen, 43-45
strawberry, 56-58, 61, 70
strawflower, 49
sumac, 39
summer savory, 70, 80
sunflower, 44, 48, 70, 83
Sunset Strawberry U-Pick, 56-58
sweet basil, 74 *see also* basil
sweet cecily, 80
sweet flag, 94; variegated-leafed, 98
Sweet Valley Herbs, 75-77
tansy, 83
taro, 96
tarragon, 80
tawny daylily, 5 *see also* daylily
Taylor, Gail, 93-95
Telford, Barbara, 20-21
thyme, 5, 80, 83
tomato, 70

Toth, Brenda and Richard, 26-28
trailing lobelia, 39
trees and shrubs, 6-18
turtle leaf, 5
University of New Brunswick, iv
Upper Gagetown, 20-21
valerian, 5
vegetables, 63, 71; recipes, 70-71
verbascum, 79-80
veronica, 5
Village Historique Acadien, 113-115
violet, 5
Visbach, Thea, 68-70
Walker, David and Susan, 56-58
water gardens, 92-99; kit, 99
water hyacinth, 95
water lettuce, 95
water lily, 96; rhizomes, 97
waterfall, 98 *see also* water gardens
watering, 4, 22, 34, 55
weeping caragana, 14
weeping mulberry tree, 14
weigela, 39
Welshpool, 29-30, 32-34, 45-46
Whalen, Judy and Bill, 23-25
white garden, 102; annuals, 103, 104; perennials, 103; trees and shrubs, 104
White, Mary, 46-48
white mulberry, 14
Wiggans, Ted, 64-65
Wilcox, Vivian, 41-43
wild columbine, 91
Willet, Phyllis, 9-10
willow, 39
winter protection *see* overwintering
Wisniewski, Larry, 1-3
Woodsmoke Farm Perennials, 20-21
yarrow, 5, 47, 83, 91
yellow loosestrife, 5, 37, 39 *see also* loosestrife
zinnia, 39